D1202936

the High Calling of Motherhood

The High Calling of Motherhood is an important contribution to understanding the importance of a mother's role in the life of the family. Everything I look for in a parenting book is here: specific, practical and doable tips and ideas, the importance of the heart, and above all the centrality of the gospel. Read it and get one for a friend!

—Tedd Tripp

Author *Shepherding a Child's Heart*, Conference Speaker

Thank you Chimene, for reminding all moms of the privilege and high calling of being a mom. All moms have dreams for their children but this book reminds us of the enormous responsibility to love, instruct, and help each child be all God intends them to be. *The High Calling of Motherhood* is written in a way that will cheer moms on and encourage them in the day-to-day work of raising their children. It reminds us that the work is not wasted but is of great value. God isn't asking moms to be perfect but to be moms who give all that they are to Him, including our daily successes and mistakes, so He can accomplish great things in our children's lives.

This book is a great shot in the arm for all moms.

—Lon and Brenda Solomon

Senior Pastor, McLean Bible Church; Washington, DC

I have had the privilege of knowing Chimene Shipley Dupler for over 35 years. From a kid growing up in a Godly family, to raising a Godly family herself, Chimene lives out the message of what it takes to be a great mom and raise great kids. In *The High Calling of Motherhood* we find what every parent is looking for, real practical insight and help in how to do the thing we all care about the most—making our kids great. From my own experience, I can say that Chimene lives out what she preaches and teaches. I encourage you to not only read this book, but to believe it and do it yourself. In a world where we are all desperate for real role models, I want to commend to you Chimene Shipley Dupler and her new book *The High Calling of Motherhood.*

—Jimmy Seibert
Senior Pastor, Antioch Community Church; Waco, Texas

The High Calling of Motherhood is an exceptional book that reminds women how privileged they are to be given one of the most powerful and influential callings a woman can have: Motherhood. Early in the book, Chimene asks a great, relevant question, "Are you embracing motherhood?" Understanding the calling of motherhood means first understanding that you are chosen by God for this calling. As imperfect as we are, we are the perfect choice to be the parents of the children God gave us. This book esteems the role of Mother in our culture and encourages us to be bold in our position as we embrace the magnitude of being called to raise up a generation of world changers. Chimene's timely and revelatory book beckons women to examine how they see their call to motherhood. Chimene's book is full of truth and wisdom and we highly recommend every woman . . . married, single, young or old to read *The High Calling of Motherhood.*

-Todd & Blynda Lane
Lead Executive Senior Pastor, Gateway Church; Southlake, TX
Women's Conference Speaker and Mother of 3 World Changers

Chimene captures the joys and challenges of being a mom as she amplifies the high calling of motherhood. She knows that mothers can experience fear and insecurity when they compare themselves to the expectations of others, which is why her heart's desire is for every mom to find their identity in Christ alone. Mothers will enjoy Chimene's candid remarks, real-life stories, and how every page is filled with hope and authentic "passion for moms" everywhere.

-Jay and Lydia Mathis
Pastor for Preaching & Vision, Grace Church; Waco, TX

It has been the greatest joy of my life to be called "Mom" for almost 19 years! *The High Calling of Motherhood* is an invaluable resource that reignited my passion for motherhood after a season of significant loss. It is easy to lose sight of the specific calling God has placed on our lives as Moms, and yet this book offers Godly advice to keep our mission and role in proper perspective. Through the wisdom and insights in this book, you will regain a passion for the greatest calling on your life: Motherhood!

—Stephanie Meeker
Mom

the *High Calling* of *Motherhood*

CHIMENE SHIPLEY DUPLER

AMBASSADOR INTERNATIONAL
GREENVILLE, SOUTH CAROLINA & BELFAST, NORTHERN IRELAND

www.ambassador-international.com

The High Calling of Motherhood

© 2017 by Chimene Shipley Dupler

ISBN: 978-1-62020-582-2

eISBN: 978-1-62020-657-7

All names and stories are true and being used with written permission. In a few instances, names and stories have been created by the author to use as examples. These examples are not reflective of any one person or circumstance.

Unless otherwise indicated, Scripture taken from THE HOLY BIBLE, NEW INTERNATIONAL VERSION®, NIV® Copyright © 1973, 1978, 1984, 2011 by Biblica, Inc.® Used by permission. All rights reserved worldwide.

Scripture marked KJV taken from THE KING JAMES VERSION, The Authorized Version.

Scripture marked ESV taken from The ESV® Bible (The Holy Bible, English Standard Version®). Copyright © 2001 by Crossway, a publishing ministry of Good News Publishers.

Cover Design and Page Layout by Hannah Nichols

eBook Conversion by Anna Riebe Raats

Author photo by Allison Kuykendall Photography

AMBASSADOR INTERNATIONAL

Emerald House

411 University Ridge, Suite B14

Greenville, SC 29601, USA

www.ambassador-international.com

AMBASSADOR BOOKS

The Mount

2 Woodstock Link

Belfast, BT6 8DD, Northern Ireland, UK

www.ambassadormedia.co.uk

The colophon is a trademark of Ambassador

To my three princesses:

Reagan, Jordan, and Riley.

I love being your mom!

You are daughters of the King.

You are world changers!

ACKNOWLEDGMENTS

The High Calling of Motherhood ended up being the heart and soul of everything I would pass on to my three princesses. Motherhood is truly a gift, a gift straight from the Father-heart of God that allows us to see the beautiful redemptive story He offers us. May we fully understand and grasp our purpose to know Jesus and make Him known. May we become intentional in raising up disciples in our homes that fully understand who they are in Christ. May we live with a passion and purpose to be calculated in the high calling of motherhood. My desire is that you, the reader, along with my three princesses, will embrace the role of motherhood with a soberness of the responsibility as well as the joy that comes when investing in the life of your child.

If we can reach the mother, we can reach the family; and if we reach the family . . . we can change the world. My prayer is that we would be intentional and purposeful with the gifts (our children) God has given us, raising up a godly generation that will influence not only this generation, but generations to come. Mothers, you are a world changer. You are a difference-maker. You are raising world changers.

I am humbled and honored that the God of the Universe would entrust me with my three daughters, my princesses, Reagan, Jordan, and Riley. Investing in them and seeing them as world changers creates in me an urgency to know God and make Him known as I want to share the joy of my salvation with my three girls. I love my three princesses with all my heart, and I desire for them to experience the joy of motherhood. Reagan, Jordan, and Riley, you are world changers! Go change the world with the love of Jesus. Thank you, Jesus, for allowing me to be a mother.

Todd, my prince charming, you are my rock. You are a faithful and loyal supporter, leader, and encourager that challenges me and inspires me. You love me well. I love doing life with you.

Dad and Mom (Don & Narciada Shipley) thank you for staying together. Thank you for choosing Jesus. Thank you for loving me and cheering for me always.

This project began with a prayer. A prayer that the Holy Spirit would use this book for His glory. I am so incredibly honored and grateful to the men and women who walked this journey with me, allowing me to share my heart for motherhood. First and foremost, a special thank you to Dr. David Vanderpoel "DV" who has walked this entire journey with me putting pen to paper. DV, thank you for investing your time and wisdom and helping me transform what was in my heart into book form. I am eternally grateful for your leadership and wisdom. Thank you for investing in me and our family. Thank you for being my mentor and most of all my friend.

Lauren Hammond, thank you for the hours of editing you gave to help transform this manuscript into a clear, heartfelt call to mothers around the world to be intentional in the high calling of motherhood. You knocked it out of the park!

To the team of mothers, all from different backgrounds and life experiences around the country, thank you for taking the time to read this manuscript and ensure that I was on the right track to deliver a message of hope and encouragement to mothers everywhere. Having the perspective of a variety of mothers in different life stages of marriage and parenting was invaluable. Thank you: Melondee Carrozza, Meg Cox, Wendy Duke, Catherine Henderson, and Francie Winslow. Jane Hampton Cook, thank you for sharing your wisdom and wit as I put the final touches on the book.

Ambassador International and Tim Lowry, thank you for the opportunity to share my heart for the high calling of motherhood. I am truly humbled and grateful for this opportunity and pray that this platform will shine the love of Jesus well. Thank you, Anna Riebe Raats, Hannah Nichols, and Brenda Covert, for your expertise in getting this work ready for publication. To the entire Ambassador International team, thank you.

And to all of my volunteers and mothers I have the opportunity to pour my heart and soul into with the Passion4Moms ministry, thank you! I love doing life with you as we are investing in the future by blessing, encouraging, and inspiring mothers in the high calling of motherhood. We are leaving our handprint on this generation and generations to come as we are raising up world changers for Jesus!

—Chimene Shipley Dupler

President/CEO

Passion4Moms

www.passion4moms.org

Contents

FOREWORD

TWENTY-SEVEN HUNDRED YEARS AGO, the fashion of the times was very much like our own. The prophet Isaiah witnessed his own people engaged in sinful folly: "You turn things upside down! Shall the potter be regarded as the clay, that the thing made should say of its maker, 'He did not make me'; or the thing formed say of him who formed it, 'He has no understanding'" (Isaiah 29:16 ESV)?

The people of Jerusalem had embraced two delusions. The first was the delusion that God did not create them. As a result, they insisted that He had no right to command them.

The second delusion was that their own understanding determined reality. They deluded themselves by thinking that they understood things better than God.

In *The High Calling of Motherhood*, Chimene Shipley Dupler rejects such false conceptions by insisting that we describe and define things the same way that God does in His Holy Word. The truth of Scripture, not the opinions of the world, must frame the way we think. As God's Word occupies our minds and affections, it will furnish our habits, strengthen our resolve, guide our thoughts, and inspire our actions.

The psalmist extols the Lord God who "gives the barren woman a home, making her the joyous mother of children." He rejoices in the truth that "children are a heritage from the Lord, the fruit of the womb a reward." *The High Calling of Motherhood* stands with generations of mothers by embracing the same sense of reverence and thankfulness for children that characterized such biblical matriarchs as Sarah, Rachel, Hannah, and Elizabeth. It is a thankfulness that needs to be reaffirmed in every generation. It was the finding of grateful joy in the gift of children that inspired Kate Douglas Wiggin, the author of *Rebecca of Sunnybrook Farm*, to start San Francisco's first free kindergarten in 1878. A few years later, Kate and her sister established a training school for kindergarten teachers espousing this truth: "Every child born into the world is a new thought of God, an ever-fresh and radiant possibility."

Now, more than a century later, such statements are regarded in many quarters as woefully out of step with the present state of affairs. Children are often perceived as a burden rather than a blessing. They constitute a distraction from, an interference with, and an encumbrance upon, the business of life—a business that is rarely defined but resolutely centered upon self. Our antinomian culture does not do well with anything that conveys a sense of restriction. Both marriage and children are viewed in that vein.

Concurrently, other voices warn us that the times smell of sunset. Society seems bent on pushing the boundaries of degradation. Base things are exalted while the holy is debased. How is it possible to chart a course in a world where everyone looks at things upside down and pronounces them right side up? It is a world where good is called evil and evil is called good, where reality is determined by the perceptions of the creature and not by the word of the Creator. Surely, they contend, it would be a cruelty to bring children to such a time and place.

In the midst of such disparate clamor, *The High Calling of Motherhood* rouses us to remember that our times, and all times, are safely kept in God's hands. And though our time finds us east of Eden, God's command to "be fruitful and multiply and fill the earth" remains normative. Its purpose for blessing has not been abrogated. The gift of each child is a profound work of God. Because of Mary's Child, motherhood is eternally exalted. Through mothers God is preparing a church to praise Him, a church that will reflect the brightness of His glory. It is indeed a high calling to nurture and care for those who are called to be immortal splendors, to shine forth with the radiance of the sun in the presence of the High King. This high calling is underscored by Solomon, who expressly exhorts us to "forsake not your mother's teaching," which he describes as a "graceful garland for your head and pendants for your neck."

Our Lord tells us that opposition from the world will be the rule, not the exception, for the people of God. Chimene underscores this when she declares that "there is an actual battle between good and evil, and we need to know which side we are on." She aptly describes our situation: "God instituted the family. Satan wants to destroy it." She then fortifies us with the inescapable logic that: "If God spoke the mountains into existence, then God can move the mountains." Nothing is too hard for God, and He has promised to be with us and for us in all the circumstances of our lives. As Chimene puts it: "Culture says post your problems on Facebook or call a friend, but God says, 'Come to me. The battle is mine.'"

The superscription that introduces Proverbs 31 reads: "The words of King Lemuel. An oracle that his mother taught him." In *The High Calling of Motherhood*, Chimene challenges every mother to consider the oracle that she will teach to her children. She reminds us that "Our impact has an eternal significance. We were made to thrive, not just survive as wives and mothers." Susannah Wesley's son, John, thrived because of her influence: "I learned more about Christianity from my mother, than from all the theologians in England."

The High Calling of Motherhood is a book that recognizes the significance of every moment. Right now counts forever. Each moment embraces all moments because it flows into and touches eternity. Chimene Shipley Dupler calls mothers to greatness in the cause of Christ, to fashion a new tomorrow by their presence today, to know God's strength perfected in weakness, and to answer God's standing challenge: "Call to me and I will answer you, and will tell you great and hidden things that you have not known" (Jeremiah 33:3 ESV).

—David Vanderpoel, PhD

Headmaster, Trinity Christian School of Fairfax

Part I:

The Orphan: Motherhood Abandoned

As I sat across the table from her one warm spring afternoon in Washington, D.C., we enjoyed catching up on life, eating our crisp Caesar salads and warm cups of French onion soup with the nation's monuments providing a beautiful backdrop. Professionals hustled and bustled their way down Pennsylvania Avenue with a mission and purpose like ants on a sidewalk. Some talking on phones and others hailing a cab, everyone seemed caught up in the busyness of life. The cafe was especially crowded that day. Sitting under a large red umbrella enjoying the deliciously warm sun, Laura, a middle-aged mom, and I shared stories and laughed as we caught up on the happenings in our families.

Quickly our conversation turned to the ever-demanding stress of trying to keep up. Laura, a successful attorney, had a daughter who just entered high school and a son in middle school. The family lived the typical metropolitan life, juggling work, school, ballet, and lacrosse while staying active in their local church. Laura had spent all of the last year filling out applications and attending meetings to ensure her daughter got into their prestigious school of choice for her high school years. Her daughter was in a ballet company downtown and practiced five nights a week. Her son was playing lacrosse on his middle school team and had just been invited to join a travel team in the community as well. Then there was Laura's career. While Laura loved working, it was just another added pressure for performance in order to provide a certain lifestyle that was expected. There was the pull of doing it all. While she wanted to work, she felt guilty for missing her daughter's ballet recitals. Now that her daughter was in high school, it felt as though the days were moving at the speed of a freight train that couldn't slow down or be stopped. She barely made it to any of her son's games due to rush hour traffic. She loved her family. She loved her job. She loved having both, but some days seemed harder than others. If only she could make time stand still.

I admired Laura. She was a good mom who loved her family well. But that day Laura admitted to me that it was hard. It was hard to juggle her professional life and to be fully present as a wife and mother. She often wondered if she had made the right decision in keeping her career after the kids were born. She had become increasingly dissatisfied with the amount of time she was spending at work, knowing that the days left with her kids at home were coming to an end all too rapidly. Most days she fell into bed exhausted but unsatisfied, believing she could have done more. As I listened, I found I could relate to Laura. There is an unspoken rule that we should somehow be able to have it all as a mom—and make it look easy.

Later that same week, I sat down with Rebecca over coffee. She began to describe her teenage son who was suffering from depression and feelings of inadequacy. His grades were dropping. He felt like he didn't fit in. His therapist had given him a label.

My heart broke for her. Why should any child, so young, feel so much pressure to perform? I sat quietly and listened as I wondered how we had gotten to the place in society that we measure success by comparing ourselves to others. Her son, now in weekly therapy, had a mom who not only felt guilty but was also sustaining a growing problem instead of getting to the root of the issue. You see, there was so much more going on that explained the depression. There were challenges at home. My friend and her husband were barely still together. Arguments and fighting had replaced a peaceful home environment. Taking her son to therapy was easier than having to deal with the bigger problems directly.

My friend was struggling too. Rebecca had started taking antidepressants just to make it through the day because the depression was so bad. She was struggling to hold it together. She sat quietly wondering if her marriage would even survive. As she took another sip of her warm vanilla latte, she whispered, "I feel like such a failure," and fought back the tears. She questioned out loud how she ended up at this place with her marriage crumbling and her son in therapy. She questioned her ability as a mom.

I think my friend knew in her heart that her son's depression and feelings of inadequacy came from a deeper place than not fitting in at school. His grades simply were a reflection of the unstable home environment. While therapy was helping, the fact that the home life was in shambles was the real issue. But instead of addressing the hard stuff, it became easier to put a bandage on and cater to her son by enabling him. She began buying him anything and everything he wanted. She tried to put him in more sports and other activities outside of school. My friend was at a loss. She herself felt insecure, inadequate, and depressed. She looked at her other mom friends who appeared to have it all together and ached for peace, but there was none. All she knew were feelings of loneliness, isolation, and anger. The polite smile and quick reply of "Everything is great!" was nothing more than a defensive mechanism of self-protection, believing that she wasn't measuring up.

And then there is Katie. Katie is a mother of four, two boys and two girls, with ages ranging from six months to eight years old. She left her job six years ago to be a stay-at-home mom. Although she loves being an SAHM, the days get really long. She feels as though she is losing her identity. When I first met Katie at a mom's group, she was the bubbly but honest one who admitted to lying in bed at night wondering if what she does as a mom makes a difference. She doubted if what she is doing as a mother even matters. "Does God even care that I am a mother?" she boldly questioned. Although she is dedicated to being at home, she feels like she is struggling to survive. Most days she feels guilty—guilty for not doing more. Guilt and a lack of a sense of purpose have left her hopeless.

At her monthly mom's group, Katie feels like she is inferior to the other moms who seemingly have it all together. She loves her kids, but she admits quite frankly to feeling like they are more of a burden than a blessing on many days. The fighting and arguing over whose turn it is to play Xbox has left her home anything but peaceful.

Her kids fight constantly. She said most days she considers herself a referee more than a mother. When she looks at other moms, she feels incomplete, insecure, and completely out of control. Diapers, potty training, and homework leave Katie questioning her sanity.

When I met Katie at a park one humid summer afternoon so our kids could play, she told me that she honestly feels like a failure as a mom. In tears, she admitted that staying at home wasn't all that she thought it would be. Summers were the worst! She found it easier when they were all occupied in sports or camps outside of the house. It seemed the only time she experienced any peace. But, of course, that meant there was guilt for not wanting to spend more time with her kids. She questioned her identity as a mom. She has simply become their chauffeur, bouncing them from one activity to another in order to keep them occupied. And so it is no wonder that each month Katie shows up at her mom's group feeling discouraged and dissatisfied in her role as mother.

Moms are depressed. Kids are depressed. Teenagers are out of control. Toddlers are running the home. Moms live life and parent from a place of constant guilt, always feeling the need to do more. We are trying to juggle a career and home life. We want to have it all. We are overcommitted and still unsatisfied. We are constantly looking to see what other moms are doing on Facebook and Pinterest instead of making our own memories. We feel we never measure up. Insecurity and fear rule our hearts and minds. Staying busy with activities is easier than the alternative of having to deal with one another at home. We are all hoping that no one will notice just how messed up and insecure we are. We have lost our sense of purpose and identity in this role we call motherhood. Motherhood is hard.

A 2014 report released from the Barna Group revealed that women fighting to "have it all" are also inundated with stress. Too much stress in life describes 72 percent of all women and 80 percent of moms. Seventy percent of moms say they are tired. Sixty-two percent of working mothers are dissatisfied with the balance of work and home life. More than half of all moms admit to being overcommitted. The struggle of motherhood is real. In fact, in this same study, 95 percent of moms say they would like to do better in at least one area of life.

As moms, we are in a constant state of struggle and inner turmoil in our daily lives. We are not at peace, but instead we are inwardly at war with discontentment and dissatisfaction either in our roles as mothers, as wives, or in our careers.

In this same study Barna states, "Moms rank family as their number-one priority and report that it's also their top time commitment. Seven out of ten say family takes the lion's share of their time—and no other commitment comes close." This survey reflects four separate nationwide studies conducted between May and August 2013. Working moms experience the greatest disparity between their priorities and time commitments. While they rank career last on the list of their priorities, it is second on their list of time commitments.

Barna Group goes on to point out, "While most moms with kids at home say they are satisfied with their family life (61%), for many it's also the greatest source of stress." The study goes on to reflect that only thirty percent of moms feel like they get adequate rest each night. Twenty percent of moms are stressed to the point of physical illness. This is twice the amount as those

> But motherhood has always been hard, in every generation and in every culture. Mothering is hard because it comes from the heart.

surveyed that are not mothers. The juggling act of balancing work and home only complicates the stress mothers experience as they feel overcommitted both at work and at home. Thirty-one percent of moms say they have too many career commitments. Twenty-six percent of moms feel they are spread thin at home.

We live in a culture of comparison and immediate gratification. Our insecurities are only compounded by social media. We report our best parenting moments and post the cutest picture of date night. We only include the Christmas-card-worthy photos from our over-planned family outing and never mention the fact that it ended in tears and silence. Just like the rest of our culture, we share a carefully crafted snapshot of our lives and leave out the rest. And so we fall into a comparison trap and become paralyzed by fear that we aren't doing it right. Instead of honestly sharing our own concerns or calling to check-in on a fellow mom who is hurting, we have neglected real, personal interactions and too often do this thing called "motherhood" alone. Motherhood is a hard road, and many of us feel inadequate, ill-prepared, and ill-equipped to do it well. But motherhood has always been hard, in every generation and in every culture. Mothering is hard because it comes from the heart.

The role of motherhood has been devalued in our society, which only complicates the inner turmoil moms struggle with today. The high calling of motherhood has been abandoned. We no longer value and esteem mothers and the impact they contribute to society as we

> Motherhood is, indeed, a calling—a high calling.

are raising up the next generation. Our culture has encouraged us to dismiss any inconvenience, whether through divorce, abortion, or even denying the time it takes to be intentional in our parenting. We keep ourselves busy and our kids in activities so that we don't have to invest in our children's lives. Anything that requires work or sacrifice is not valued in our society unless it provides satisfaction or recognition. This has become the norm.

We have lost the meaning and purpose of motherhood and the responsibility that comes with the high calling and gift that it is. We have forsaken it as a spiritual matter and used it as another stroke for our own ego and advancement. Motherhood has been orphaned and disdained by our culture. Instead, we rejoice in our self-entitlement and celebrate freedom from responsibility. We don't want to be inconvenienced or burdened. And we definitely don't want to have to work harder than necessary. This have-it-all culture of self-entitlement and convenience is the antithesis of motherhood. Yet, if we truly intend to raise up a generation of world changers, the calling of motherhood must be resurrected with a call to action by our society.

Motherhood is messy and hard. But it is also a gift. We are leaving a legacy. We are impacting the culture and the future. We are leaving our mark and handprint on society. To do so, we must be intentional and purposeful. That begins with understanding our own individual purpose as mothers. Motherhood is, indeed, a calling—a high calling.

Chapter 1

THE GIFT OF MOTHERHOOD

I LAY IN THE DARK, in the stillness, in the quietness, on a less than comfortable hospital bed. It was my first time in the hospital. I had never been sick. My only visits to a hospital room were to visit others. Now, I was the patient. Yes, we were "those" parents who had researched everything and had arrived with a long list of "do's and don'ts," should there be any complications during my labor and delivery. But now I certainly didn't know what to expect as I lay there holding my firstborn daughter, just hours old.

Before my daughter was born, I had been working on Capitol Hill in the United States Senate. I loved the excitement of life on the Hill. It is a unique place that has a fraternity of its own. I loved being a part of that fraternity and the inner circles of those making a difference in the world. It was always entertaining to go back to my friends and family in Texas and realize that "Inside the Beltway" wasn't just an expression but a real way of thinking that you just couldn't explain to anyone else. My time on the Hill was a special time, full of fond memories and relationships.

I thrived and continue to thrive on having a plan and leading a busy and rewarding life. While I love politics, I personally never had any political aspirations. My one and only aspiration in life from the time I was very young was to be a mom. So when I became pregnant and the time came to turn in my key from the young, hip, idealistic, professional world on the Hill, I was happy to do so. I know not every woman is wired to be a mom from day one. But I was! Many of my friends have grown into the role of motherhood. Many of my friends happily juggle a professional career and the world of mothering. Yet I knew that while I loved walking the halls with congressmen who were literally making decisions that affected the entire world, I had a different mission. So, I packed up my desk, turned in my key to the Russell Senate Office Building, and began my adventure as a mother. I was eager to begin this journey. I was overtaken and enraptured with an uncontainable joy. I beamed with a giddy smile knowing that I had been awarded the title of "mom."

These were the thoughts and feelings and memories that I was experiencing as I lay in that hospital room in the serene quietness of the night. All my dreams had come true as I held a 7 lb. 8 oz. baby girl with jet black hair and big brown eyes. She was perfect. Reagan.

But something came over me that I can't fully describe or explain. There was a pain, a conspicuous pain that I immediately felt take over my body as I held my little girl. Nothing had happened. Nothing had gone wrong. Everything was perfect. But what was this pain? My rock star husband, Todd, had slept in the car throughout the night just to be nearby. There wasn't room for him to stay with me in the hospital room, and he didn't want to leave me and drive the 45 minutes back home. So he slept—or didn't sleep—in the car. He came in as soon as possible, around 6:00 AM, and I told him about this pain I was experiencing. It wasn't a physical pain. It was an emotional pain. I quietly whispered as I looked down and smiled at my baby girl and said, "I didn't know love would hurt this much."

I was in love.

This love was my first glimpse at the intensity and love of motherhood. It was nothing I could have prepared myself for—it only arrived the moment I held Reagan in my arms. I think every mother and father experiences this kind of unspeakable, unexplainable love at some point in parenting. It is why we fight to protect our children. It is why there is so much competition even among parents in their willingness to go to war with anyone or anything that would harm their child, whether physically or emotionally. We become crazy people when it comes to protecting our children. We are like the lion who lies calmly basking in the sun until one of her cubs is in danger, at which point she roars fiercely and loudly, willing to die fighting to protect her young. We are the same way as parents. So I lay there tightly holding my baby girl, less than twelve hours old, and was overtaken with a love that literally hurt . . . I felt it!

As we were discharged from the hospital, we were given pamphlets and brochures about caring for our infant daughter, everything from nursing tips and formula samples to basic information on infancy. I sat in the back seat of our Ford Expedition as Todd drove Reagan and me to our little apartment in Alexandria, Virginia. We walked up the flight of stairs and were home at last. We were a family of three. I was in love. All my dreams were coming true. I was a mother, and I had my baby girl to hold and love and watch grow.

The responsibility that parents have to care for their child can be daunting. New parents, especially, read so much, and there is so much fear associated with all that could go wrong. I read every pamphlet we were given because everything was new. I wanted to be educated. I wanted to know my options. I wanted to do what was best for my daughter. Maybe it is because mothers often feel overwhelmed with the idea of caring for a new life that the hospital really only prepares you for the first few weeks of life. This initial education consists of the basics of survival and protecting this new life. But the reality is that there is so much more to motherhood than simply survival. And no one fully prepares you for all that lies ahead.

Our journey as a mother is so much greater than those first few weeks of surviving sleepless nights and the required feedings every three hours. There is so much more to embrace in the adventure beyond decorating a nursery and attending playgroups. The reality is that motherhood is so much bigger than all of that. We often walk into motherhood with a dream of creating a family neatly packaged among beautiful strollers, designer diaper bags, and monogrammed onesies, but the phenomenon is so much more. Ensuring that our sweet little baby is fed, diapered, and clothed is just the tip of the iceberg. Motherhood, that great responsibility of raising a child to be the man or woman God intends them to be, has just begun. We have been given a gift. As a mother, we can impact a life. We can raise up a world changer.

> We can raise up a world changer.

I don't look down on my friends who entered into motherhood kicking and screaming. And I don't judge my friends who seem to juggle motherhood and a professional career so gracefully. Currently, I am a working mom too, trying to navigate a professional life amidst carpool and homework. I respect every mom in every circumstance! It is important to understand that this book is not about a "right" way to be a mom, but instead how to embrace the role of motherhood as a gift from God. So often I hear moms say, "I am just a mom," as if her role is less important than the woman with a professional career. Motherhood is more than a job. It is more than a title. It is a calling.

Mary, the mother of Jesus, was handpicked by Almighty God Himself to be the mother of Jesus. Wow! Can you imagine the overwhelming emotions Mary must have experienced? She must have been awestruck that she was chosen to be the mother of the Son of God! That is a breathtaking thought: the idea that God, sitting on the throne in heaven, would personally call out this young girl, saying, "I choose you."

Mary didn't have any notoriety. She wasn't special. She was plain and ordinary. She was just doing life as a young Jewish girl, and then God sends an angel and is like "Oh by the way, you should know you are pregnant with the Son of God." Talk about having weird dreams or maybe having too much wine the night before!

The irony is that we are all chosen, and we are all called. While, yes, Mary was chosen to be the mother of Jesus, it is no accident or happenstance that God has also chosen you to be the mother of your children. Just like Mary, you were chosen! You have been handpicked by God Almighty to be the mother

> Our God is an intentional God.

of your children. You were chosen to be the mother to the very children that you call your own, whether biological or through adoption. It has been known and planned by God from the foundations of the earth. Our God is an intentional God. The gift of motherhood is not an accident. There has been no mistake. You have been chosen and called to be the mother of your sons and daughters.

There is so much detail in the intricacy of cells coming together to become a human life as each child is knit together with such care and attention in our wombs. With that same precision, God gave you the exact children He planned for you from the foundations of the world. Being chosen adds an extreme soberness to the responsibility we have as mothers. God is entrusting us with the care and training of our children. When we stop long enough to let that marinate, we can understand more fully the honor and responsibility we have been given by God Himself.

Mary was human, a sinner. And yet, God chose and equipped her with everything that she needed to be the mother of Jesus. Likewise, you and I are fallible humans who have been equipped to raise the children that God has lovingly placed in our care. If God chose me to be the mother of my three daughters, then He is going to provide me with the resources that I need to fully care for them as unique individuals. The challenge becomes looking to God alone for these tools for success, not our culture and not other moms.

Ephesians 4:7 says, "But to each one of us grace has been given as Christ apportioned it." One definition of grace is "favor or honor." This means that by being appointed, I have His favor. I am favored by God. I have been chosen with the honor of being a mother. I am fully equipped to be able to parent with God's grace. I have been called with a purpose and have been supplied with the grace needed to carry out that calling. But, I must look to Christ to walk boldly in that equipping and calling. He is my lifeline and source for successful parenting. If God is the giver of life and loves my daughters more than I possibly can, and I have been fully equipped to love and train them well, why would I look to anyone but God? All the resources are already available to me. He has made them available, but I must learn to look to Him alone if I intend to walk in the calling of raising up world changers.

We have been handpicked for our roles. For me, this increases my obligation and ownership of my role as a mother. By being personally chosen, that means I am accountable. Therefore, I have a responsibility to do my job well. I can't be concerned with comparing myself to other moms and how they are raising their children. Just like Mary, the mother of Jesus, was called and chosen, you, my friend, were called and chosen. Motherhood is an honor. It is a responsibility. It is a gift. Motherhood is a high calling from God!

One of the careers I always dreamed about having was to be an OB-GYN. I never went to med school or ventured down that path, but this was one career that always fascinated me more than anything else. I love everything about pregnancy and birth. I love that a new life is growing inside of a mother's womb. The idea that each detail of a person's makeup, personality, color of eyes and hair are being put together so intentionally is nothing short of a miracle. A heartbeat and internal organs that are working together to allow life outside the womb is remarkable. Life is a miracle. I find it all completely fascinating and one of the most beautiful parts of life that we as women get to take part in. I know many women will find this hard to believe, but I have always said that I would give birth every single day (so long as there's no back labor)! I just absolutely love everything about pregnancy and a new life entering the world. I loved giving birth! It truly is one of the most beautiful miracles.

I remember the first birth I ever witnessed. During college, I was a volunteer in the newborn nursery at a hospital. It was one of the best experiences of my life! The day I got to see a new life take her first breath as she emerged from her mother's womb was truly one of the most beautiful things I have ever witnessed. Seeing life come forth, knowing that God Almighty had been witness personally to every detail of this infant, taking an interest in every organ, vein, and design that makes that individual unique, was absolutely amazing. To stand and watch new life enter this world was a joy that I will never forget.

One of my absolute highlights while working in the newborn nursery was being the first to bathe the daughter of one of my best friends. Arrangements had previously been made for my friend Jay to call me when Lydia went into labor. So when I received the phone call one cold February morning, I rushed to the hospital and quickly made my way through the securely locked door. I changed into my blue uniform and scrubbed in, fully washing well up to my elbows. As I walked into the newborn nursery, I was elated! One of my closest friends was just down the hall giving birth. I was going to be the one honored to give her daughter her very first bath. The nurses wheeled the infant cart down to the nursery while a gathering emerged just outside the nursery window. There stood the proud new father, Jay, along with his parents and mother-in-law. I was on the other side of the glass, picking up my dear friend's newborn daughter, Lawrie, a beautiful baby girl with jet black hair. I was overcome with honor and ecstasy giving a newborn, just minutes old, her first bath, gently washing the vernix from her skin. After the warm bath, I diapered and swaddled her, ready to return her to her mother's arms. This was a moment I would cherish forever.

By the end of college, I had witnessed a natural childbirth, a C-section, and a circumcision. I held newborns just hours old and had given countless first baths. I carefully walked the halls, returning newborns to their exhausted but radiant mothers after the babies' first visits to the nursery. More importantly, however, I was developing an enduring love and appreciation for motherhood. Life is beautiful. Life is a miracle. Life is a gift from God.

The Bible so perfectly describes God as the Creator of life in Psalm 139. He is personally involved in our design and makeup. He is the Creator of this beautiful gift we call motherhood. "For you created my inmost being, you knit me together in my mother's womb. I praise you because I am fearfully and wonderfully made; your works are wonderful, I know that full well. My frame was not hidden from you when I was made in the secret place, when I was woven together in the depths of the earth. Your eyes saw my unformed body; all the days ordained for me were written in your book before one of them came to be" (Psalm 139:13–16).

It feels as though the moment when a newborn enters the world, God Himself is personally handing us a beautiful and perfect gift— life. It is as if He is offering a gift, an opportunity, for us to personally have a part in another human being. Life that He took the time to create in a mother's womb, He is allowing us to care for. Motherhood is a gift to be cherished.

Often the joy of motherhood vanishes when we don't fully grasp the value and significance of the influence we have in motherhood. We get caught up in a culture of comparison and self-serving gratification, neglecting to understand the mission of motherhood. We wrestle with the antithesis of motherhood in our culture. But if we truly believe that life is created by God, then we must fully understand why we are created. Why do we exist? What is our purpose and mission in being called to the gift of motherhood with the opportunity to invest in the next generation?

> We exist to glorify God, and our purpose is to know God and make Him known.

Genesis 1:27 describes how we were created in the image of God. As such, we should reflect Him in our lives. Revelation 4:11 states, "You are worthy, our Lord and God, to receive glory and honor and power, for you created all things, and by your will they were created and have their being." All exaltation and praise should go back to God as the giver of life. We must not exalt ourselves in our creation. Our existence is from the Creator of life, God Almighty. "For in him all things were created: things in heaven and on earth, visible and invisible, whether thrones or powers or rulers or authorities; all things have been created through him and for him" (Colossians 1:16). We were created for His glory, not our own glory. He has created and authored life for His glory and His purposes. It is not about me. When we are living to exalt ourselves (which is what our culture tells us to do), we are not fulfilling our purpose. We exist to glorify God, and our purpose is to know God and make Him known.

Therefore, my life as a mother should also reflect the image of God and bring Him glory. The same is true for our children. The lives that we have been given the opportunity to touch and influence, their lives have been created with that same purpose and design. They, too, have been created in the image of God and for His glory. As mothers, understanding and knowing our purpose in being created allows us to fully participate in the calling of motherhood.

When we understand that we are created for God's glory and that life isn't about us but about Almighty God, it shifts our perspective and our entire worldview. We understand that our place of influence as a mother is to raise up a generation that understands that their purpose in existing is not about themselves but about knowing God and making Him known. That we have a place of influence to impact the next generation changes how we parent. When we understand that our mission and purpose should be to glorify God in everything we do and say, pointing our children to Him, we have a new urgency in how we parent and live out motherhood. The gift of motherhood takes on a whole new meaning when we grasp the realization that life is a gift from God and we have been chosen by God Himself to be image-bearers of who He is. We have been given a gift to reflect God and share that joy with the lives He has entrusted in our care.

As I recognize that I was chosen and given the gift to person-ally impact and influence another human life, all for the glory of

God, this absolutely changes my entire framework on motherhood. I am no longer concerned about anyone else giving their stamp of approval on my performance as a mother. My lifeline and equipping is vertical, not horizontal. I am keenly aware that this gift of motherhood is for God's glory—not my own and not for others. He cares for our children and loves them more than we ever could, and yet He has entrusted us with a role in this great journey. That is an awesome responsibility! We have been given the distinct honor to hold, love, and teach these precious children. He is allowing us to have a voice and place of influence in their lives. I am handpicked and chosen by God Almighty, who sits on His throne, to be a mother. Motherhood is a gift to bring God glory.

Chapter 2

THE WORLD OF SOCIAL MEDIA: INSECURITY AND COMPARISON

PEW RESEARCH CENTER IS A nonpartisan research "fact tank" in Washington, D.C. Their research brings to light issues, attitudes, and trends shaping America and the world based on research and public polling. Pew Research released a report, "Parents and Social Media," in July 2015 based on a study conducted in September 2014. The report stated that "Social media is broadly viewed as a source of useful information and as one parenting tool among a collection of options. Mothers use it as a parenting resource slightly more often than fathers."

Moms, obviously, spend a lot of time on social media these days. In fact, we rely on social media to make decisions on everything from discipline ideas to medical opinions to the best entertainment for our children. We are living in a culture of immediate gratification for answers to the questions we have at any given moment in time. We can literally put our kids down for a nap and by the time they wake up, we have been able to get advice from social media on what park to take our kid to that afternoon, what to make for dinner, and the best practices for sleep training our little one who still isn't sleeping through the night. We can communicate with anyone across the globe, research any subject matter, and post everything that we did that day for friends and family to feel like they are a part of our kid's childhood. In this same study, Pew Research states, "Mothers are heavily engaged on social media, both giving and receiving a high level of support via their networks."

Pew Research goes on to conclude that "seventy-five percent of parents use social media for some kind of parenting information or social support." Of those online mothers, eighty-one percent use Facebook. Other forms of social media used by parents are Pinterest, LinkedIn, Instagram, and Twitter, with Pinterest at forty percent of mothers.

We live in a world of easy communication where we can both share and request information and receive instantaneous responses via social media. For the most part, this is a luxury our culture and generation has come to enjoy. Everything is at our fingertips. In addition to social media, there are apps for everything on the mobile devices we carry. On them we can find a plethora of answers to any of our questions within seconds, whether it is what is the highest rated vacuum cleaner or reviews for the restaurant we have been wanting to try. Information is readily available in our world today.

While having easy access to gaining information is a perk, social media also contributes to moms playing the comparison game. Social media has become a breeding ground for insecurity among moms.

Then, on top of that, consider the insecurities that women struggle with just by virtue of being a woman. I mean we are the most hormonal, emotional, judgmental creatures ever created. We love to compare, tear-apart, and eat our fellow species of women alive. Add that to today's world of social media and you have a mom's perfect storm for feeling like everything she chooses to do or not do is dangling out there for judgment.

If you are a mom, I know you know exactly what I am talking about. It starts early. There is comparison from day one with the kind of birth experience you are planning, and all sides hold fast to the position that their way is the right and only choice you should choose. There are reasons why you should or should not have a home birth, go to a hospital, use a midwife, opt for an induction or C-section, or have an epidural or no epidural. Then, once your little bundle arrives, you are now faced with the rights and wrongs of your choice to breastfeed, use a bottle, or (heaven forbid!) use formula. You and your baby haven't even left the hospital and there are already ravenous women on both sides ready to eat you alive and tell you why your choice is clearly right or wrong. As your kids get older, the pressure to provide lavish, over-the-top birthday parties will send every mother into competitive mode. And it doesn't stop there.

Insecurity and comparison are the enemies of every woman. It is human nature that we measure ourselves against others to determine success and failure. We have all been there. As young mothers, it is like an unspoken race for success on how early your baby learns to crawl, walk, talk, and read. There is a tinge of pride when we know that our child is outdoing the baby next door. There are the polite conversations at playgroup about what your baby is doing this week, which either spark feelings of pride or inadequacy. You know what I am talking about. I was recently observing two young moms comparing stories on social media. Amanda, a first-time mom, was beaming with pride when her daughter began to move from scooting across the kitchen floor to full on crawling. She posted a video on Facebook, politely announcing to family and friends this milestone of success. Not to be out done, Britney, also a first-time mom from Amanda's playgroup, immediately remarked that her daughter was almost there, and oh, by the way, her daughter was now sleeping through the night. There was something in Britney that felt a little sting when Amanda's daughter was the first to mark this milestone of crawling. It is amazing how quickly milestones turn into competition. Whether it is crawling, taking a first step, losing teeth, or reading before preschool, we are all eager for our child to be the one excelling. As mothers we tend to turn everything into a competition to make ourselves feel more successful in our role of mothering. By posting each activity and milestone on social media, we get noticeable accolades and more strokes of approval for all to see.

In contrast, moms of high school kids are begging for life to slow down, knowing that their little ones are about to leave the nest. They tell young moms to cherish each day and enjoy the moment. They know all too well that time goes by too fast. And yet, because we have a need for affirmation from others, we use our children as pawns, pushing them to reach milestones as a way for us to look good to others. We torture ourselves with this kind of comparison. While there are some legitimate milestones that all children should be achieving in their childhood, it doesn't have to be a race to see who gets there first. Unfortunately, we as moms are the ones who are encouraging and perpetuating this kind of measuring.

Our obsession with social media has contributed to moms feeling more alone rather than supported or encouraged. Our culture of posting every event, thought, and moment can make one feel isolated. When you are scrolling through Facebook or Instagram, you are looking at a collection of different moments out of context all at one time. Your brain tells you that all of these things are happening while you are at home doing nothing. The collection of posts tell you that you are not out making special memories with your children, your husband has not brought you flowers and treated you to a romantic dinner, you are not at the beach or on vacation at Walt Disney World, and you are still driving the same car and living in the same house with stains on the carpet. You can scroll through social media, and while each person may have a special event or happening that day, our brains are interpreting it as a whole. We are seeing a collective of events from different people all taking place at different times, but it reads that all of this excitement is happening now, and we are the only ones not a part of it. We must remember that what we are really looking at is a highlight reel of someone's very best moments.

If we are not careful, these brief interactions with other people's highlights can leave us feeling empty, lonely, and depressed. We begin having feelings of inadequacy and not measuring up, based not on fact but on perception. It is important to note that while we know these events are the highlight reels of a person's best moments, emotionally we can interpret these happenings negatively as we are reading them as a whole. This can be a very real battle for moms in the culture we live in today, where we expose everything and where we live very outwardly for "likes" and validation from others. When we thrive on approval from others, we begin eagerly anticipating and planning the next Facebook post in our mind long before the actual event may occur. We become obsessed with finding affirmation in something that is not even personal. Living life this way, with highs and lows based on approval from social media, can lead to depression, especially when that approval never comes and we are left disappointed. This leads to isolation and the feeling that the culture has abandoned us in our roles as mothers. Depression is a real struggle for many moms.

The juxtaposition of our own lives with others outwardly lends itself to feelings of isolation inwardly. This isolation creates a space for moms to feel very abandoned emotionally—orphaned by our society instead of supported and encouraged. Oftentimes, we feel like we aren't measuring up based on an unfair perception of reality. We are constantly playing the comparison game, which leaves us feeling very alone and inadequate. Instead of having other moms cheering us on, we feel like we are constantly being criticized or having to defend any decisions we make as a parent. Feeling like we don't measure up leads to feelings of failure. We have been told by society that we aren't good enough if we can't juggle a career and motherhood—having it all. Yet none of us can truly have it all—not alone, and not without help.

> We have been told by society that we aren't good enough if we can't juggle a career and motherhood—having it all. Yet none of us can truly have it all—not alone, and not without help.

I often talk with mothers who have left high-powered positions in the workplace. Many of these moms struggle with the choice to stay at home with their children. I recently spoke with an attorney who had chosen to leave her place in the corporate world to spend time at home with her preschool children. Later, when her kids were old enough to begin school, she chose not to return to work like she originally planned but to remain at home. As she described her feelings of insignificance when she would go with her husband to his work events, I recognized that her situation was not at all unique. Compared to the line-up of career women in suits, she felt inadequate. Questions flooded her mind, such as, "Have I made the right choice to stay home?" Like other women in her situation who have chosen to give up the powerful corner office to stay home and organize carpool, they question whether it all really matters. "Would I be more satisfied in that corner office, providing more financial support to enable us to take more vacations and giving our children more unique opportunities?" In today's culture these are questions that plague women constantly.

On the flip side, I've sat down with numerous women who are still in the office interacting daily with people of influence, carrying the burden of late nights at the office and after-work "happy hours" while missing their child's soccer games or those priceless after-school conversations. These women feel guilty for dividing their time, missing ballet recitals while representing clients.

On paper, it looks like we can have it all. But the reality is we all have the same number of hours in a day, and how we fill our twenty-four hours is a personal choice. The question is less about whether you choose to work outside the home and more about what kind of time are you giving your children when you are with them. This choice comes down to what is right for each individual family. The pressures are real. The struggle is real. And there is sacrifice with both decisions. We honestly *can't* have it all. Something has to give.

I work from home, and yet I still find myself answering emails or taking conference calls instead of sitting down to a board game with my child or having a conversation about her day. We all make sacrifices and choices. With each choice come sacrifices, either in time or money or both. Instead of being quick to judge a fellow mom, we should be more concerned about how we can encourage a mom to be successful in the role of motherhood and do that well, regardless of whether that includes working inside or outside the home. The role of motherhood is a high calling and one not to take lightly, so the bigger conversation should be how we can encourage moms to be intentional in their roles as mothers regardless of their professional choices.

Let's also address our single moms before moving forward. The fact is that there are a plethora of moms who are single, whether by death or divorce or choice or other circumstances beyond their control. Single moms, you are doing a great job! The road is hard and even more complicated in your journey. May we all learn to be kind to one another in the journey of motherhood.

Single moms and married moms alike, we have a responsibility to embrace our role as a mother. We must learn to support and encourage one another, knowing we are impacting this generation and generations to come. All too often we are looking to motherhood to find fulfillment and identity. We must stop looking to motherhood to find our identity. And instead of creating discord and identifying success by how we juggle our many roles in motherhood, we must look to embrace the role of motherhood itself, which has value and eternal significance.

Comparison and envy of birthday parties, designer clothes, and Christmas presents feeds women's covetous wants and desires. Moms now ostentatiously arrive at playgroup or at school in their luxury, fully-loaded SUVs ready to show off their status symbols, but they still leave with a twinge of jealousy after comparing themselves and discovering new ways in which they don't measure up.

Oh, and then there is school. There is the competition of what school your child is attending, what accelerated classes they are taking, what sports they are playing, and how successful they are in their academics and extracurricular activities. Social media only perpetuates the contending for who is ahead as you post pictures of your child's 4.0 earned while also making the travel sports team. Your self-esteem as a parent is being determined by whether you appear more successful on Facebook, by what vacations you are taking, what new car you are driving, and how your child is excelling in school and on the court or field.

The problem is we are creating and living in a culture plagued by never feeling fully successful. We can't keep up. Even the seemingly most flourishing women—those who appear to have it all together financially, in their marriage, their appearance and wardrobe—are struggling behind closed doors. We live in a culture that is more quick to rip you apart than to come alongside you and be a team player supporting you in your role as a mother. It is out of our own arrogance, insecurities, fear of failure, fear of success, and need for approval that we feel it is okay to tear every other person to shreds so that we can stand on top like we have conquered the world.

Comparison robs us of our joy. There is a passage in Ephesians that talks about unity in the body of Christ. "I urge you to live a life worthy of the calling you have received. Be completely humble and gentle; be patient, bearing with one another in love. Make every effort to keep the unity of the Spirit through the bond of peace" (Ephesians 4:1b–3). Of course, this passage in Scripture refers to brothers and sisters in Christ living in unity, endeavoring to keep the peace as fellow believers. But what if we look at this passage as mothers? If God has entrusted our children to our care, do we not have a responsibility in this calling? If we are to live a life worthy of the calling we have received, and motherhood is our calling, should we not make every effort to find unity and keep the peace? As we are called, we should live a life worthy of the calling, reflecting the image of God and bringing Him glory. As we work toward unity as believers in Christ, we should seek to be completely humble and gentle and patient with love for our fellow mothers.

Instead of ripping one another apart because our parenting styles look different, we should find ways to encourage one another. Our standard of success should not be one another. We must keep our eyes vertical on God who called us to motherhood instead of measuring success horizontally with fellow mothers. We will constantly feel inadequate and small when we look to others to determine our success. When we look to social

Fear breeds insecurity. Insecurity breeds comparison. Comparison takes our eyes off of Jesus.

media to determine our status for success, we are seeing only a small window into the reality of another family's true life. A mom will gladly post all the fun outings with her kids but will leave out that her marriage is falling apart and crumbling. We must get to a place of understanding that perception is not always reality. Our benchmark for success must shift from others to God.

Fear breeds insecurity. Insecurity breeds comparison. Comparison takes our eyes off of Jesus. We have it all wrong when we mark success by looking to each other instead of God's benchmark for success. When we look to flawed, sinful, imperfect human beings as our benchmark for success, something is off. We believe Facebook to be reality and truth. We believe the lie that the mother who posted on social media has no problems. Instead of keeping our eyes on God, the giver of the gift (our children), we are looking to the right and left, the front and back, at everyone and everything, but we have taken our eyes off Him. We must remember that our children, these blessings, are His. He should be our benchmark for success.

Often in our search for identity as women, we look for significance in places such as our career, our appearance, our homes, or even through our children and our role as a wife and mother. We long to be told we are successful and doing a good job to secure our identity, and yet we live life in regret and guilt when we are successful in one area of our life while another area suffers. Stay-at-home moms can be there physically but may not be fully present mentally and emotionally.

Regardless of your decision to work or be at home 24/7, the bigger question remains: Are you embracing motherhood? Do you take pride in it, or do you sheepishly say, "I'm just a mom"? You are not JUST a mom. You are chosen! You are blessed. You are called. Our identity must shift from comparison to confidence in who we are in Christ. Our identity mustn't be found in our children. Rather, we must find our identity and confidence in Christ.

> Our identity must shift from comparison to confidence in who we are in Christ.

My approval and favor comes from God—not our culture, social media, or other moms. Yet, too often we get caught up with the rules of comparison of how we are supposed to be a mom rather than just enjoying being a mom. Living in the world of comparison paralyzes us from living and living well. But the insecurity and comparison tend to fade away when we realize the duty we have before us in the assignment of our own children. Not only have we all been created as unique individuals, but God has also handpicked each one of us to care for our specific children. Recognizing this gift and responsibility makes me more vehemently aware of my obligation to successfully raise the children that I am called to influence. My job as a mother becomes my own priority, and I can't compare myself to you and how you are doing as a mom. I begin to learn to navigate how to stay in my own lane. I have been chosen and entrusted with *my* kids, not your kids! I have been appointed to them, not you. I am chosen. I have an opportunity for influence. We must stop comparing, and we must begin running in our own lane and own it.

Chapter 3

MOTHERHOOD ABANDONED IN OUR CULTURE TODAY

FOR OVER TWENTY-FIVE YEARS, I have been working in some capacity with families, both professionally and in volunteer ministry. Studying and serving the family with a concentration in marriage and parenting have become my passion. Whether through working with married couples, coaching moms one-on-one, or working with kids in social work, my time has been centered on the family unit, studying and observing the importance of the role of motherhood.

Early in my career, I had the opportunity to work with children and see the family from a child's perspective. During these years, I worked with children who had been abused, neglected, and had some of the most horrific stories you could possibly imagine. I was surrounded by children who had anything but a normal and healthy childhood. There was physical neglect of the basics, such as even living in a proper home that would provide shelter and care. While we take for granted that every mother would care for her child's basic needs of food, clothing, shelter, and affection, that is not always the case. Sexual abuse within and outside the home was far too commonplace. There is nothing that surprises me anymore. Nothing! Spending my days in the foster care system, in the special education system, and in institutions for children who had been removed from their biological families, my eyes were opened to an entirely different kind of perspective on motherhood, or the lack thereof.

I was the child's advocate and friend. I had to learn how to build a relationship with each one of them because the people who should have loved and cared for them had lost their trust. When a child can't count on his own mother and father, how can he ever fully learn to trust anyone again? They have experienced loss and a warped sense of what a home should be. Having been robbed of a loving childhood, these children grow up with a very misguided worldview of what a family should even look like and carry with them more baggage than any child should ever know. This baggage and distorted worldview on what a family should be is now part of the next generation. How did we get to this place? I quickly learned that we do not all enter the world of motherhood from the same worldview or perspective, but all children still need and desire a mother to provide not only the basics of care but also unconditional love and support.

Most recently, my last fifteen years have been spent working with other moms directly. Once again, this offers a different perspective and vantage point in understanding the impact of the role of a mother. Now instead of a child's perspective, I am working first hand with mothers themselves, gaining access into how they process and understand their role. Through speaking engagements with mom groups, coaching moms one-on-one, being a mentor mom, and overseeing my own non-profit ministry for moms, I have talked to and counseled hundreds of moms.

Looking back, I can clearly see God's plan for me and my passion for moms. Not only did He prepare me from an academic point of view by equipping me with a Bachelor of Science Degree in Child & Family Studies, but He also provided me with the opportunity to learn from both a child's perspective as well as from a mother's perspective. The years of varied experiences, some born out of pain and some out of joy, have been an education on the importance of the family unit and the impact the family has on society. Through firsthand observational experience I've learned that motherhood is a very integral and critical role not only in each child's life but also in society as a whole.

One of my favorite kids to work with was a young girl we'll call Mia. She was a tough girl in middle school. She rarely smiled, and when she did, it was mostly a smirk conveying her negative thoughts about you. The disintegration of her family left her abandoned and orphaned. It wasn't death that made her an orphan; it was the breakdown of the family that left her abandoned. She had scars on her wrist from cutting herself. She had been sexually active. She put on such a front of being mean and hard to ensure that no adult would approach her. But, for some reason, we connected. I was finally able to break through the wall, and Mia gradually began to talk to me. She trusted me enough to share not only about her day but her feelings as well. She had been abandoned. She had been neglected. She had been abused. She had lost her sense of purpose and belonging. Mia had built a thick wall around herself for self-protection and self-preservation. Her heavy eye makeup helped her feel safe and strong.

But the pain was enough that she tried to take her life on more than one occasion.

Our society is full of kids like this. The fragmentation of the family that Mia encountered is becoming all too familiar. We enter into marriage and start a family, but when we don't value marriage or emphasize the role of motherhood, we begin to lose an opportunity for influence with our children. Often our own brokenness is carried over into our parenting. We don't enter into the role of parenting with a skill set for survival, much less success.

The lack of respect for motherhood in our culture today has created an abandoned and orphaned state for the role and job of a mother. Our society has devalued and castrated the calling of motherhood to a place of second-rate citizen and not something of a worthy or noble calling. We have fallen for the lies that being a mother is insignificant and that it really doesn't matter—it's just something you do. It is not revered as a gift or a privilege—much less a calling. It has simply become a box to check. You grow up. You go to college. You get a job. You get married. You have kids. It is just something we are expected to do as adults. We have bought into the lie that it is meaningless and insignificant outside of our own satisfaction. This is compounded by our culture no longer respecting or valuing traditional marriage and the unique roles and differences of a man and a woman. The role of motherhood is unique and different from the role of a father. Both roles of a parent, mother and father, are significant and needed but serve very different purposes.

An orphan can be described as *isolated* or *abandoned*. In the previous chapter, we discussed how the comparison trap can lead to feelings of tension and isolation. The perceived "togetherness" via social media leaves mothers at home feeling alone and inadequate. We add "friends" to our Facebook page after one brief encounter to give the perception we are well-liked and have a plethora of friends. It becomes the adult version of a middle school popularity contest. The reality often is misguided. Due to seemingly being engaged and aware of happenings thanks to "status updates," we consider ourselves "caught up" on life and yet we haven't spoken to anyone. We are aware of facts and have knowledge, but we are not engaging with each other. This leads to feelings of abandonment, leaving mothers orphaned in society and realizing that what we have is superficial and not anything meaningful.

Additionally, our culture is abandoning the role of motherhood as we ourselves feel entitled and are bringing up the next generation to also expect entitlement. Even as mothers, we don't want to be inconvenienced. We are self-serving and expect immediate gratification. We drive through Starbucks for our extra hot, no-foam vanilla latte on our way to the gym where our trainer is waiting to give us our personalized training regimen. When we get home that evening after our kid's sports practice, we place an order on Amazon Prime that will be waiting on our doorstep the next morning. We don't even have to go to the grocery store and wait in the check-out line any longer. Instead, we can place an order online and have our groceries delivered to our door. We have come to demand immediate results; waiting is no longer an option. Anyone or anything that slows us down or gets in our way is a nuisance. We are raising an entitled generation that demands success and an easy life at all turns. It starts somewhat benign in enjoying comfort but moves all too rapidly to demands for entitlement. This is starkly reflected in our attitudes any-time we are made to wait. What begins as small requests of "deserving" moves quickly to much larger, life-altering demands. It is from this place of self-serving, self-gratifying mentality of convenience that many women feel entitled to abortion rights. We are breeding a generation that is consumed with self with absolutely no thought to our neighbors or a common courtesy for others. We care only about ourselves, regardless of the effect to others, including those in society as well as our own families. It is from this place that many have bought into the lie that we are entitled to abortion to ensure that no woman will ever be inconvenienced.

Another way motherhood has been orphaned by society is the cultural shift that views motherhood negatively. If we take a look back in history—whether it is the "good ol' days" of the 1950s or all the way back to biblical times—the role of a mother was esteemed. Even in years gone by, while women fought for equality in the workforce and our culture, there was still a dignity associated with motherhood. Mothers were still protected and valued. In our current society, however, we have embarked into a new day where the impact a mother has in the role of the family is no longer valued or respected by society. We no longer embrace the influence of the mother/child relationship as one of lasting significance.

I personally place much of the blame on us as women who have fought so hard and desperately for liberation and equality with men that we no longer revere or think highly of the unique roles God gave us as women. We have so wanted to be treated equal to a man that we no longer treasure the exclusive roles we are given as a woman. Our culture no longer values the difference between men and women.

We no longer value marriage. We no longer value motherhood. This cultural decline, I think, is unique to our generation and something we have not faced in generations past. It has been a gradual and subtle change that has made us more comfortable and desensitized to negative consequences of this revolution.

This decline in our society has nothing to do with equality. It has nothing to do with equal pay or equal job opportunities, etc. I do believe in equal pay. I do believe in equal opportunities for women. I am a woman, and I want those equalities for myself and my daughters! However, I also believe I am a distinct creation and that God bestowed unique gifts and abilities to me as a woman. I think differently than a man. I am wired differently. We need to learn to accept and appreciate the beauty of these differences, as opposed to trying to become the differences. When we lose respect for our identity, our marriages, and our role as women, it directly affects the role of motherhood in our culture.

Our culture has given the joy of motherhood a bad name. We moved from the 1970s when women demanded equality with men to now having a generation that no longer embraces or values our identity as mothers. We, as a culture and society, have abandoned and neglected the role and calling of motherhood. Motherhood is orphaned by society. This is a spiritual issue. Motherhood is a spiritual calling. And we have abandoned this calling. The orphaned state of motherhood is reflected all too clearly in the families in our society today. Marriages are falling apart. The biblical covenant of marriage is no longer valued and esteemed. The family is no longer valued. Children are no longer valued. According to the most recent report from the National Right to Life, there have been 58,586,256 abortions in the United States since 1973. We are a generation that is completely okay with throwing away the gift of life and the gift of motherhood that God so graciously offers us. When we flippantly toss out and kill many lives, gifts from God, without a second thought, it is clear that human life is no longer treasured in our society. This is not a belief or decision that is forced upon us but rather an ideological choice that we, as mothers, are choosing to embrace and crave as an entitlement. A disrespect for human life and decline in the value of traditional marriage is evidence that the role of motherhood is clearly not revered or respected. This all directly impacts our role as mothers. The problem in our culture is that not only does our society not value motherhood but also that we as moms don't value motherhood ourselves.

It is easy to point our fingers and blame culture. We can blame a shift in traditions and times, and we will always be able to point back to history and say things are different. Things will always be different. Times will always change in every generation and in every culture. Yes, culture does and will affect how we view our roles. But should culture be our benchmark for success? What about the church? Has the church supported and esteemed the role of a mother with honor, dignity, and value? What has the Christian community done to embrace the role of mothers? Have we too bought the lie that we are "just a mom"? While the culture and social media do affect how motherhood is perceived and received in our society, what are we doing to rise above that and not fall into that trap believing that lie?

We, as a society, have abandoned the calling of motherhood that God established. But God has never left. His calling has never changed. His purpose and plans have always been the same. We are the ones who have left and walked away from this calling and purpose. If we go back to the very beginning, the Bible says, "So God created mankind in his own image, in the image of God he created them; male and female he created them. God blessed them and said to them, 'Be fruitful and increase in number; fill the earth and subdue it'" (Genesis 1:27–28a). Later in Genesis, God told Noah, "Be fruitful and increase in number and fill the earth" (Genesis 9:1b). From the foundations of the earth, God has instructed mankind to be fruitful and multiply. God created man and woman with the calling to reproduce and build the family. Since we have been created in the image of God, our lives should be a mirror and reflection of God. Our children should be a reflection of God. God intended for us to have children. He is the one who created the role of the mother. He is the one who gives life. God is the one who opens and closes the womb (Genesis 29:31; 1 Samuel 1:5, 19–20). The idea of the family and role of motherhood originated with God and His grand design for creation.

However, our culture does not value traditional marriage. We do not revere marriage as a spiritual issue and a covenant relationship that God deems holy and sacred. Additionally, the idea of getting married is on the decline as couples favor cohabitation. Marriage is no longer a cherished relationship, but rather we settle for cohabitation with the intent to determine compatibility. In fact, a recent study by the Barna Group reported that sixty-five percent of Americans believe in cohabitation and believe it to be "generally a good idea." The study goes on to report that forty-four percent of adults would approve of their children cohabiting before marriage.

Furthermore, the study concluded,

Living together before marriage is no longer an exception, but instead has become an accepted and expected milestone of adulthood. Even a growing number of parents—nearly half of Gen-Xers and Boomers, and more than half of Millennials—want and expect their children to live with a significant other before getting married. The institution of marriage has undergone significant shifts in the last century. What was once seen as primarily an economic and procreational partnership, has become an exercise in finding your soulmate. Where once extended families lived within a handful of miles from each other, now the nuclear family often strikes out on its own. Such shifts placed a new emphasis on marriages as the core of family life and revealed fault lines in many marriages. These pressures, along with a number of other social phenomena—including women's growing economic independence—led to unprecedented divorce rates in the second half of the twentieth century. As a result, many of today's young people who are currently contemplating marriage, see it as a risky endeavor. They want to make sure they get it right and to avoid the heartbreak they witnessed in the lives of their parents or their friends' parents. Living together has become a de facto way of testing the relationship before making a final commitment.

Ironically, we have also learned that "people who live together before marrying divorce at about twice the rate of couples who do not cohabit before marriage, and four times the rate if they marry someone other than their present partner." This is according to a study by Marripedia, an online social science encyclopedia for topics on marriage, family, religion, and sexuality. The shifts occurring in our culture are weakening the institution of marriage and moving it farther away from the covenant relationship that God created to be holy and sacred.

The lack of respect for the role of motherhood is a reflection of our society. The decline of the family institution—including the rejection of traditional marriage, rise in abortions, and an overall disdain for the biblical worldview of marriage and the family—are a reflection of why motherhood has been orphaned and abandoned in our society and culture today.

In the Bible, the first family consisted of Adam and Eve and their children Cain and Abel. Before Cain acted upon his anger and sinned by killing Abel, God spoke to Cain. "But if you do not do what is right, sin is crouching at your door; it desires to have you, but you must rule over it" (Genesis 4:7b). God warned Cain that sin wanted to take over his heart and that he must be prepared and tame it. Unfortunately, Cain chose not to master the sin and killed his brother out of jealousy. Satan will always seek to destroy our marriages and families. Sin will always be close by. Sin is crouching at all of our doors, and Satan desires to rip apart our marriages and families. But God warns us to master it. We must know our own hearts and our weaknesses.

> While we parent from a place of sin, the redemptive story of God can be told through our families.

In our relationship with Christ, we have the fruit of the Spirit, a product of our relationship with Him. We are called to bear fruit for His kingdom. When we have the fruit of the Spirit, it is an overflowing of the relationship we have with Christ. Likewise, our marriages—an illustration of the relationship between Christ and His bride, the church—are a covenant that is a picture of forgiveness and unconditional love. It is an intimate love relationship that also bears fruit. It is out of the love and covenant relationship of marriage that two come together as one and produce children. Our children can be a spiritual reflection of unity and fruit from the covenant relationship of marriage. While we parent from a place of sin, the redemptive story of God can be told through our families. The family has the opportunity to reflect God's great love story to a lost and dying world. God created the family because God cares so deeply for the covenant of marriage. Children are a beautiful reflection of the love story of marriage.

We must be the ones in our culture to embrace this calling. We must understand the impact and potential we have as mothers. When we can fully understand and embrace our roles and potential as mothers, our entire worldview on motherhood will shift. We will never look at motherhood the same. We as moms must change our worldview and begin to embrace motherhood as a high calling. We must understand and fully own that the role of motherhood, while orphaned by our society, is not orphaned by God.

Part II:

Changing our Worldview: Embrace the Calling of Motherhood

So often women feel they must stop *living* when they become moms, like suddenly all of their freedoms are gone. This is especially true after the births of multiple children, when our bodies tell us that we aren't the women we used to be. When running and playing with them, we can't keep up with our children like we once could. We can't even hold our eyes open past 10:00 PM. But, truth be told, I think that women should *begin* living all the more when they have children.

When you are a mother, you have a part of you imprinted all over this child to invest in and share the joys of life. Now is the time to start living! It is now, when we have children of our own, whether biological or through adoption, that we have an opportunity to affect another life. Motherhood allows us to share the joys of dancing and singing, as well as holding our children tightly when they cry or scrape a knee. Now is the time we can shine as women as we teach our children about life and the world around them. As mothers we get to be a teacher, nurturer, mentor, coach, disciplinarian, nutritionist, accountant, mediator, chef, chauffeur, snuggler, nurse, advocate, friend, counselor, role model, stylist, and more. We have an immeasurable list of ways and opportunities to invest in the lives of our children that we will never have in the corporate world or any other job. Being a mother, simply put, is the biggest job out there with the most responsibility because we are investing in lives. Our roles as a mother are vast, and those moments of teaching and listening have the opportunity to impact the future! Our opportunities as moms will literally shape and mold another human being all by how we use our title: MOM!

We have the privilege to embrace the high calling of motherhood with an enthusiasm and expectation that we have been given the gift of influence to shape and mold the next generation. We can leave an imprint on society and on culture. We can be world changers by raising up a generation who influence the world for Jesus in a bold way. It is so easy for us to become internal in our thinking instead of external. Mothers can leave a legacy that will live on for generations to come. The power of our influence as a mother has the potential to change the trajectory of our culture and the next generation. That is a powerful point of impact! Not only do we have the opportunity to invest in our children, but by being intentional with our own families, the scope of influence also exponentially widens for generations to come.

As we begin to understand that we have been chosen in the calling of motherhood and that our children are a gift from God, we will begin to parent from a place of passion and purpose. The intensity of this calling on our lives will begin to burn in us a desire to make the most of every opportunity. We will begin to cherish every moment of influence, knowing that it is a gift. Psalm 90:12 will become our prayer, "Teach us to number our days, that we may gain a heart of wisdom." As we begin to shift our worldview to a biblical worldview and mindset, we will become desperate to ask God, the giver of our gift—our children—for wisdom in the mission of how we parent.

Knowing that I have a voice of influence in the lives of my children, I'm compelled to have a correct worldview, as I have the truly awesome responsibility of helping to shape and mold the framework of my children's thinking. I am called to teach them right from wrong, to love them, nurture them, and give them a foundation for living life in this great big world. I get to be that special person. I am called. I am chosen. No one else gets that kind of influence in my children's lives. Motherhood doesn't just matter; it makes a difference.

> The biggest challenge in our culture is that we don't view our role as mothers with an eternal perspective.

As moms, we often can't see past the days of nursing, diapers, and sleep deprivation to the long-term and lasting effects that we will have on our children. Unfortunately, we do not live in this missional mindset that the work we are doing now directly impacts the future. The biggest challenge in our culture is that we don't view our role as mothers with an eternal perspective.

Our culture tells us that if we get our kids into the best schools, make the travel sports team, become involved in the arts, and contribute to society by giving back in a philanthropic endeavor, we are successful. The rat race of suburbia is putting our kids in all kinds of activities and keeping them busy with as many experiences in their childhood as possible. As moms, this not only contributes to but also feeds our insecurities of not doing enough. We begin to compare and perpetuate our sinful entitlement worldview. We fight for more. We are never satisfied. We live in a constant place of discontentment rather than gratitude. Our house is never big enough, we never have enough furniture, our kids need more stuff, they need to experience more, our family needs to vacation more, and even our dog needs more toys. Our culture encourages and perpetuates our sin nature of self-gratification. The world revolves around me and my needs. It is with this worldview that we are actually teaching our children to feed and grow their sinfulness rather than making them aware of their need for Christ.

Our culture and society is by nature self-absorbed, self-serving, self-centered, and self-pleasing. It should be no surprise that we are looking to anything and everything to serve our well-being and success, including our children. However, putting the pressure on our children to succeed, making them our idol, is one of the most unfair things you can do to them. They are imperfect sinners like us, so to put that kind of pressure on them to perform is unfair. Our children should not have to carry the burden and pressure to give us an identity. Our identity should not be found in our children.

Our own upbringing and childhood often prevent us from entering into parenting with an intentional game plan. We parent out of what we know. Or we swing the pendulum too far to an extreme to avoid the hurt we experienced. But what if our generation of mothers can shift that cultural worldview and understand the magnificent but sober responsibility we are given as mothers? What if we begin to parent from a place of confidence, understanding the bigger picture? You have been chosen for this job. As mothers, we need to own our place of influence and embrace it!

As we take on our calling in motherhood, we must shift our worldview to a biblical worldview. We must become more concerned about reaching our child's heart. The behaviors and actions of our children are simply an overflow of the heart. Luke 6:43–45 represents this perfectly. "No good tree bears bad fruit, nor does a bad tree bear good fruit. Each tree is recognized by its own fruit. People do not pick figs from thornbushes, or grapes from briers. A good man brings good things out of the good stored up in his heart, and an evil man brings evil things out of the evil stored up in his heart. For the mouth speaks what the heart is full of." Our actions and our words reflect what is in our hearts. What we feed will grow.

Parents can't fully be successful in reaching a child's heart for Jesus and helping our child overcome a selfish sin nature if our own hearts as parents haven't fully been captured and changed by Jesus. We need a heart transplant. We as mothers must first change before we can fully and successfully reach our child's heart.

Our culture not only has abandoned and neglected the important role of motherhood, but we also don't encourage mothers to be intentional in their role and understand their long-term impact. Mothers have an important, God-given opportunity to impact their children's lives, but it takes work and requires sacrifice.

In shifting our worldview to a biblical worldview, first we must understand that we will be going against the norm. We must realize that we will be in the minority. We won't be in the popular crowds.

Second, we must embrace the hard work that is required to be deliberate in our roles as parents. Intentional parenting requires all kinds of sacrifice, especially time. As we have noted previously, this is countercultural, as we are constantly encouraged to be self-serving in our search for immediate gratification at all costs.

And third, and finally, we must fully understand who we are in Christ, since our primary focus in parenting must be to reach our children's hearts and make them aware of their need for Jesus. We need to parent from a place of knowing that we are in a spiritual battle, not a physical battle. Parenting is spiritual. Reaching hearts for Jesus and having an eternal perspective in our parenting requires us to completely shift our worldview in how we approach parenting all together. We are not in a battle of the wills when it comes to our two-year-olds or teenagers; rather, we are in a spiritual battle. We are on a mission with the Holy Spirit to help our children understand their need for Christ. These three areas will completely transform our worldview—but this is not the culture we live in.

We must change our worldview to embrace motherhood for what it is—a calling. We must begin to parent with a biblical perspective, understanding that our children are a gift from God. We have been chosen to invest in this gift. Therefore, as mothers we must become intentional in looking to the giver of the gift, God, as our benchmark for success, not our culture and not one another. When I understand the urgency of the task before me in my own home, I become less concerned about comparing and looking to other moms for approval and accolades. Shifting our parenting model to a biblical worldview with an eternal perspective becomes my mission as I embrace my role of motherhood.

Chapter 4

MOTHERHOOD FROM A BIBLICAL WORLDVIEW

OUR CULTURE IS ALWAYS LOOKING for the next remedy. Whether it is a new weight loss program, the latest gadget to simplify life, or a miracle drug to cure what ails us, we are always looking for an easy fix for the struggles we face in this life. We would rather take a diet pill than have to avoid eating junk food or exercise. It is easier. Our society has gotten to a place of always looking for a quick fix but never really wanting to do the work or experience the pain that goes with it. We want to avoid work at all cost. We want the solution without putting in the time or effort of hard work. And we typically want the easy way out. We want to all be winners.

Too often, the kind of product that is the next "big" thing ends up being a bandage rather than a cure. We possibly can prolong the inevitable, but unless we get to the root of the problem, we will never provide a life-changing, life-altering solution to our needs. But what if we already have the answer? What if we can stop searching and begin living with success? What if that answer requires work? Are we willing to accept the hard work to get a solution that will last?

Growing up, I spent every summer and every day after school working at my dad's dental office. As I got older, my responsibilities increased. To say I am familiar with the dental world is an understatement. Growing up with a dad as a dentist, I have come to have an obsession with teeth. I love teeth. I love pulling teeth. The joke around our house is that if you are in your primary years and have loose teeth, do not tell me, because I will want to pull them. Yes, I have even pulled the teeth of my friends' kids!

But no matter how much I like dentists and the idea of teeth, if I don't take care of my own oral hygiene and don't spend the time needed to brush and floss, there are going to be some natural consequences. Let's say I get a cavity, but I don't go to the dentist because I hate them so much. I just want to ignore the problem because it is too much work to have to make an appointment and go somewhere I don't enjoy being. Obviously, the problem isn't just going to resolve itself. Not only will I experience pain as the area of decay grows larger, but I will also face the more colossal risk that infection can get into my blood stream.

What once began as an issue of being lazy and not wanting to do the work of routine check-ups and daily brushing and flossing has now become a sizable problem. The apathy in not wanting to do the work turns into an area of decay. If I simply ignore the issue, the need for a filling becomes a need for a root canal or even worse. What could have been addressed as a small problem is now a big problem. Having a root canal is a much more intense procedure than a filling.

And even worse, if I don't address what is now a root canal, I am running a major risk of the infection getting into my blood stream and having very real impact on my entire body. What was once a small area of decay that I wanted to ignore is now an infection circulating throughout my entire body via my bloodstream.

Sometimes, we know we have a real problem on our hands, but we spend a lot of time looking for a quick fix to address our child's behavior instead of getting to the root of the problem, reaching the heart. We want to put a bandage on our child's behaviors. We are quick to make excuses for their behaviors. We laugh it off, knowing inwardly we have a serious problem. We make a game of disobedience. How often have you seen moms and dads call a child to come to them, and the child runs away? This turns into a game of chase. Laughter ensues. In those situations, we are teaching the child that our words don't matter and obedience is optional. We begin teaching them that when we call them to obedience, we will play along with a game of disobedience. What happens when there is an emergency and I call my child to come for her protection, but she responds with the expected game of chase and it turns dangerous? It starts early. Just like those small areas of tooth decay, if we don't begin with healthy habits in the early years of parenting (first-time obedience, respect, care and concern for others, etc.), bigger issues will arise as our children grow older.

I am constantly amazed at the number of parents who are literally intimidated by their toddlers. Since when are two and three-year-olds scary? But the look that the parent gives when a toddler says "No" is one of sheer panic; the parent doesn't know how to handle the situation. I am often around parents who let their toddlers control their every move. When the toddler says "No," the parents are the ones who are obeying instead of the other way around. The parents are quick to give in to a toddler's demands, cowering and acknowledging the toddler's every wish. You may laugh, but this is true! It happens all the time. A child-centered family is the norm in most homes in our generation. And this is exactly how we end up in this kind of child-centered family role. We allow our children to dictate from a very early age who is boss and who is in control. And when we allow our children to choose roles, *of course* they will choose to be the authority on any given subject.

Like many moms, I joined a mom's group when my girls were young. It was a church group for first-time moms with a leader who was to be a resource for wisdom and encouragement. There was one particular winter morning that I will never forget. I was pregnant with Jordan, our second daughter, and Reagan was about eighteen months old. Although very young, she was old enough that I expected obedience for a simple request. As the mommy group was ending, we helped pick up toys and made our way to the door. It was a cold winter day, and I had her small navy pea coat ready to put on her. I sat Reagan on a small wooden bench next to the door and began to put the coat on her, one arm at a time. She began to fuss and refused to put on the coat, pulling her arms away, determined not to wear her coat. As I knelt down to get on eye level, I told her that she needed to wear the coat. As Reagan continued to fuss, the leader of the group began to laugh and made some remark about typical kid behavior and was it really worth the effort. Her response implied that if Reagan didn't want to wear a coat, why bother?

Now, trust me, I have been in very uncomfortable and awkward situations when a child is being disobedient and the parent is embarrassed; laughter somehow feels like the natural thing to do to alleviate the uncomfortable moment. However, in that moment, I was actually very disappointed and frustrated that this was the response of the "leader"—she was supposed to be encouraging us in our roles of motherhood!

While this was a very benign incident, I learned quickly that even in the church we are not calling our children to a standard of obedience. We are not encouraging parents to be intentional in their role of parenting when it comes to training our children. While I know the leader meant nothing of it, that moment had a huge impact on me as a young mother. At that moment, I realized that I was going upstream and against our culture by being the parent who actually expected my toddler to obey. Even in Christian circles, this is not the norm. Calling our children to obedience can be a very lonely and hard road. But when we understand what is at stake and look at the long-term consequences, it keeps us focused and determined in our parenting choices.

I knew that if I wanted my toddler to obey in a very simple task like putting on a coat when it is freezing outside, then my job as the parent is to have her wear the coat. This is not done out of being a mean or controlling parent. Rather, this call to obedience is done for her own good, to protect her and train her to obey me and trust me because I have her best interest in mind. I also knew that if I let my toddler tell me no and did not require obedience for the simple task of wearing a coat, the long-term effects could be much greater when my teenager tells me no in defiant disobedience. Oftentimes, we don't parent with the long term in mind. Instead, because we don't want to get in a conflict over something as simple as a coat, we pick and choose our battles. But the problem is that we give our child the choice of picking the battles we engage in as they decide when they want to obey or disobey. We are passing the baton of authority to our toddlers rather than training them. What we do today with our toddlers will have a direct impact on what their teen years look like.

The good news is that if we do the hard work now while our children are young, the teen years will be amazing! Teenagers are a blast!

> What we do today with our toddlers will have a direct impact on what their teen years look like.

We have two teenage daughters, as well as a tween, and I absolutely LOVE them. They are the best years and so much fun. The world tells us that the teenage years are horrible and should be dreaded. If we choose to parent according to our culture and feed the self-centered desires and fail to reach the heart, then, yes, I would also dread the teenage years. However, when we are intentional to reach our child's heart early, we make them aware of their sin nature and need for Jesus, the Savior. We can then get to the root of discipline, which is an issue of the heart. We did A LOT of hard work laying the foundation when our girls were little in order for the teen years to be fabulous! It doesn't just happen.

Sometimes people say, "You have it easy because they are all girls—if only you had boys!" While, yes, there are major differences between girls and boys (once again proving that there are differences between men and women), training a child, boy or girl, is possible. We are looking to reach the heart of the child, whether male or female, making us all aware of our need for Christ because we are sinful. We must choose not to believe the lie our culture has taught us to believe—that teenagers have to be horrible or difficult. The teenage years, for both boys and girls, can be remarkable if you are intentional about putting in the time and hard work required in those early years of parenting. The payoff is monumental! Teenagers can be some of the most helpful and insightful human beings. But just like going to the dentist and being intentional, we have to be willing to do the hard work—it doesn't just happen.

Now for all the moms reading this book with teenagers who are freaking out that they didn't do the hard work in the foundational years, don't panic! It is NEVER too late! God's grace is always available and sufficient. God has given us the grace we need; it has already been allocated to us. "But to each one of us grace has been given as Christ apportioned it" (Ephesians 4:7). We can always reach a child's heart with the help of the Holy Spirit, regardless of our child's age. While there may be some repair work and drastic changes that need to be made in order to become intentional in your role as a mother, rest assured, it is never too late! Our teenagers may wear a tough exterior, desiring to become their own person, but they are desperately longing for our attention and approval. I promise you, your teenager who may appear uninterested is actually longing to spend time with you. It is never ever too late to be calculated in reaching your child's heart.

The challenge often becomes the amount of time and sacrifice intentional parenting requires. Like everything else, we want the results without doing the work or putting in the time. It is easy for all of us to want to do nothing in the evening because we are spent and exhausted from the day. We would rather watch a favorite TV show or read a book instead of taking the time for those conversations and teaching moments. And oftentimes, being inconvenienced is a big part of calculated parenting and parenting with a purpose. Parenting from a biblical worldview requires me to be intentional in reaching my children's hearts for Jesus and making them aware of their need for Christ. My job becomes helping my children to understand their purpose—to know God and bring Him glory. This requires calculated parenting 24/7 with the objective of making our children aware that they are sinners in need of a Savior. Reaching our children's hearts for Jesus is our primary purpose in motherhood. This requires a lot of time, energy, and effort in our parenting. It means we will be inconvenienced. Like going to the dentist for routine check-ups, we want to be proactive in reaching our children's hearts for Christ in order to avoid doing a lot of damage control in later years.

One spring day, my mother-in-law was in town, and we were going to spend the day together at the mall shopping. I love shopping! I think it's my love language. Reagan was very young, and the three of us were going to spend the day at the mall. It was the perfect girls' day out, a day of shopping and lunch. But not too far into our outing, Reagan began to throw a fit. She was a toddler who wanted her way that day. She was sitting in the stroller so I bent down to get on her level and look her in the eyes. I informed her that if she continued to throw a fit, we would immediately leave the mall, go home, and she would take a nap. Now, a word of advice to all parents: think before you speak! Once you make a threat, you must keep it or your kids will learn that you aren't really serious. If you say you will leave the mall, you better be prepared to leave! If you threaten to leave the mall and they fuss again and you don't leave, they will learn they can continue to disobey and you won't really follow through.

Well, let's just say my mother-in-law and I were the ones who suffered that day. Reagan continued to throw a fit and got her consequence for misbehaving. I will not be made out to be a liar; my kids can always take me at my word. So, I looked at my mother-in-law and said, "I'm sorry, but we will now be leaving." We had been at the mall for less than an hour, but we packed our bags and headed straight back to the car. Maybe I should have thought that one through more, but my kids have never ever doubted me when I tell them we will end something should their behavior not change. They know they can trust me, and they know that I will follow through regardless of how embarrassing or inconvenient it may be. Thankfully, my mother-in-law respected me, understood, and supported my decision, although we both would have preferred to shop. But intentional parenting is very countercultural and requires sacrifice. Just like taking the time to brush and floss every day will avoid decay later, being intentional in the mundane everyday moments prevents future problems down the road.

Why do you think teenagers get such a bad rap? It's not the kid's fault! It's the parents' fault for not knowing how to engage and interact with their teenager. Since the child was a toddler, the parents forfeited their rights of authority, passing that mantle onto the child. Too often in our culture today, parents are giving up their authority, allowing their young children to take the reins and control every move inside the home. But we are commanded to call our children to obedience. Ephesians 6:1 clearly states, "Children, obey your parents in the Lord, for this is right." Biblical parenting has a very clear delineation for parents and for children. In our charge as mothers, it is our duty to walk confidently in our authority and call our children to walk in biblical obedience to our authority.

A defiant two-year-old is the same as a rebellious teenager. And more often than not, the parents I work with are actually intimidated by their two-year-olds. But if we don't know how to create both boundaries for and a relationship with our children when they are young, the teenager who is seeking independence and identity will appear unreachable. We must know what we are dealing with, which is the human heart. We must understand that our role as parents, our job, is to reach our child's heart. My dad had a favorite quote when I was growing up: "Rules without a relationship lead to rebellion." We must build a relationship in order to have influence.

> We must understand that our role as parents, our job, is to reach our child's heart.

> Rules without a relationship lead to rebellion.

One of the number-one complaints that I hear from parents is that their children argue and fight all the time. Homes are not peaceful but are instead a place of yelling, screaming, arguing, and fighting. Our family was recently with another family, and one of their children out right asked my three girls if they ever fought. Of course, they have disagreements and have become quite frustrated with one another, but Reagan's response was, "Umm, no, not really." She went on to explain that, yes, as sisters they do disagree and get frustrated with one another, but that yelling, arguing, and fighting were not a part of who they were as siblings. Fighting does not define them and is not how they deal with problems. The children asking were shocked and began to make excuses for why their family fights so much. But the reality is that we create a culture of acceptance for how we deal with problems.

We as parents set the standard for what is allowed in our homes. When our children get angry, they have a choice in how they choose to react. This is what we want to teach our children. There will always be problems. The question is not IF we will have problems; the question is how to respond WHEN we have problems. Fighting among siblings is, indeed, a response to anger and frustration—but it is a choice. It is also a choice if parents permit fighting as a permissible solution in their homes. Not that there will never be a disagreement, but we must define what is permitted as an appropriate response. When parents allow siblings to fight and argue all the time, then that is a choice that helps define the home. We are training our children how to deal, or not deal, with their conflicts. If we believe that fighting among siblings is normal behavior, then we as parents are the ones choosing to allow it in our homes. We are feeding our child's sin nature if we teach them this is an appropriate and normal response.

Again, we must go countercultural and look at what the Bible says about conflict resolution. Look at Proverbs 15:1 that says, "A gentle answer turns away wrath, but a harsh word stirs up anger." As mothers, are we relying on culture to dictate our expectations and parenting choices, or are we looking to the Bible, God's Word, as our standard and source of wisdom in parenting?

My college roommate and best friend at Baylor, Ashley, would ask me every single day, "What can I do for you?" To be honest, it drove me crazy because I didn't understand her persistence in caring about doing anything for me. That kind of attitude had not been modeled for me in my home growing up. I was so perplexed by her daily offer to help me. It wasn't until I had children that I realized that this should be the heartbeat of our home. Ashley's daily question in college had a profound impact on what I wanted the heartbeat of my home to be.

We should have a daily attitude of looking for ways to bless and serve one another. What would our homes look like if we were defined by every member of the family asking how they could serve and help one another? Can you imagine walking into a home that was defined by this one question, "What can I do for you today?" Instead of our having to ask our children to unload the dishwasher, they offer to help out of a servant's heart. When we see our husband is tired from a long day at the office, we look for ways to bless him. We should be creating an atmosphere where our sons and daughters are proactively looking for opportunities to serve one another instead of fighting to keep score, tallying who has done more. If we create a culture in our homes where our children are looking for ways to bless their siblings, such as doing a chore that is typically not assigned to them, or asking what they can do to help, we will be teaching our children how to practically be the hands and feet of Jesus to others by looking for opportunities and ways to bless and serve those around them. If they can't serve their siblings or those in their own home, how can they serve others well? This changes the entire identity of our homes. This allows a servant's heart to permeate and become the pulse of our homes. When we are more concerned about others and less concerned about serving ourselves, we can change the world. This servant heart mentality was modeled by our Savior, who came to serve and not be served (Matthew 20:28). With this kind of attitude, our homes will be more peaceful. There won't be the constant arguing and fighting. We are reaching our child's heart rather than feeding a self-indulgent, self-serving spirit.

The Bible teaches us the principle of reaping and sowing and blessings and curses. There are natural consequences to sin. We must look to that biblical worldview as we are training our children to understand this principle that what we feed, grows and what we starve, dies. The Bible says, "Do not be deceived: God cannot be mocked. A man reaps what he sows. Whoever sows to please their flesh, from the flesh will reap destruction; whoever sows to please the Spirit, from the Spirit will reap eternal life. Let us not become weary in doing good, for at the proper time we will reap a harvest if we do not give up" (Galatians 6:7–9). The reality is that we as parents not only have to deal with our own humanity of sin and our own selfish desires but are also in charge of dealing with our child's selfish sin nature. The challenge becomes our desire for an easy road, feeding the sin nature because that is what is comfortable and comes naturally. Putting a bandage on our problems is the easy solution. But God calls us to a higher standard by addressing the root, the child's heart.

Cultivating a servant's heart in our children is countercultural. And yet, if we look to the perfect parent, God, and the only perfect child that has ever lived, Jesus, this is our biblical framework for parenting. They become our model, not our culture. Shifting our worldview is a challenge but necessary if we are going to reach the heart of our children. We should begin teaching our children that their greatest concern should be looking for opportunities to serve those around them, modeling Jesus rather than being so concerned about serving themselves. But unfortunately, in most cases, we are raising self-centered, entitled children who aren't even showing care and concern in their own homes.

When we begin to shift our mindset from the culture to a biblical worldview, God's Word becomes our standard. God, the giver of the gift of motherhood and our children, is the only perfect parent. Although we ourselves are imperfect sinners, we have a faultless role model we can look to for parenting. We are exhorted to "Follow God's example" (Ephesians 5:1). God calls us to have a vertical mindset, with God Himself being our only standard. Our Heavenly Father has demonstrated for us the ultimate examples of sacrificial love and forgiveness. God's mercy, love, grace, and forgiveness become our model for how we can walk in this same mercy, love, grace, and forgiveness as parents with our own children.

The only perfect child ever to live is Jesus, the Son of God. He, too, becomes our standard for living from a biblical worldview. He taught us obedience, servanthood, and accountability. When Mary and Joseph searched and found young Jesus in the temple, he returned home with them when called, walking in obedience. "Then he went down to Nazareth with them and was obedient to them. But his mother treasured all these things in her heart. And Jesus grew in wisdom and stature, and in favor with God and man" (Luke 2:51–52). His humility and servant's heart, as well as His fierce obedience, illustrate for us the standard of growing in wisdom, stature, and favor with both God and man. This is the framework for us as mothers and the standard for our children. Yet, we spend more time looking to other sinners who are imperfect rather than keeping our eyes on the

> The primary goal of missional parenting, with the intent to reach our children's hearts for Christ, is to have an influence and a voice in reaching the world around us.

perfect parent and perfect child in God the Father and His Son Jesus.

As mothers, we must cultivate our children's hearts, teaching them first to care for those in their own home before they can successfully go out and care for others in the world around them. If our children can't show love and concern for those in their own homes, how will they navigate those relationships outside the home? Home base becomes our mission ground. The change first has to occur in each of us individually as mothers. The primary goal of missional parenting, with the intent to reach our children's hearts for Christ, is to have an influence and a voice in reaching the world around us. What we feed, grows and lives. The more we feed it, the stronger it gets. We must not be surprised by behaviors based on what we are feeding and encouraging to grow in our homes. Instead, we must begin to starve our sin nature and feed our spirit and relationship with Jesus if we expect it to grow. Reaching our children's heart for Jesus is our primary purpose in motherhood.

I am reminded of the Scripture in which Jesus says, "But you will receive power when the Holy Spirit comes on you; and you will be my witnesses in Jerusalem, and in all of Judea and Samaria, and to the ends of the earth" (Acts 1:8). Jerusalem was the disciples' home base; it was where they began their mission. Likewise, when we have the Holy Spirit come upon us as mothers, our first priority is our home. We can't go out and make a difference in the world and neglect our family. Our primary mission field is home base, first and foremost.

This is a gift and honor. We have been chosen to share Jesus with our children. We are chosen and called to preach the gospel, first making disciples in our own homes. Just think of the exponential influence this intentionality could have when our children begin making disciples of their own!

There is a reason we are instructed to start at home: the potential reach becomes exponential. Oftentimes we want to neglect our Jerusalem, our home base. But if we emphasize discipling our children for Christ, the growth potential to make more disciples becomes much greater and far-reaching! If we become calculated as mothers to focus first on our own homes, then we have an opportunity to change the trajectory of the next generation.

> There is a reason we are instructed to start at home: the potential reach becomes exponential.

About ten years ago, I had decided that making a little extra money on the side would be a good thing for our family. There was a position open in a local church where I could still be home with my three girls, who were all very young at the time, while allowing me to serve on the weekends. I thought this would be the perfect scenario for ministry while bringing in some extra cash flow to assist our family. Shortly after I was hired, however, there were some changes in other staffing positions which, in turn, changed everything that had been promised when I accepted the job. I was now expected to put in hours at the local church office as opposed to doing my job from home. This would mean time away from my children.

Although disappointed, I knew that this was no longer going to work for my family. I was not willing to neglect my "Jerusalem," my three girls, in order to make a difference and share the gospel with "Judea." Now understand, I am not saying that working at a church was bad. The concept was great, but once I was no longer permitted to work from home and keep my own children as the priority, I could no longer stay in the position. I was not willing to compromise the opportunity to be home to teach my girls about Jesus. I was not willing to risk losing "Jerusalem" for "Judea." There is a time and season for everything. Maybe if my girls were older, this could have worked. But in the season of life I was in, I had to stand my ground that my family comes first. So, I resigned. Ministry is good work, but not at the risk of losing our own families. Too often we want to be in places of ministry sharing the gospel, but God gave us fertile soil right in our own homes that we are commanded to reach. We neglect the gift of making the disciples He has given us. Serving in places of Judea and Samaria are good, but not with the risk of forgetting about Jerusalem first and foremost. I believe our homes should be our primary focus of missional training and raising up disciples. Currently, I run a growing non-profit ministry that trains and disciples mothers. This requires a lot of juggling and has become my Judea and Samaria for sure. But I can never forsake my girls, my Jerusalem, in the process.

> Ministry is good work, but not at the risk of losing our own families.

Looking vertically to God the Father as the perfect parent and to Jesus, the Son of God, as the perfect child gives us a standard for parenting with a biblical worldview. While we as mothers will sin and make mistakes, we do have a perfect example set before us that gives us tools for success as we make it our mission and priority to reach our children's hearts for Jesus. Our prayer as mothers should be that our children's hearts would be captured by the heart of God. Chosen and called to make disciples, our homes are our mission fields. Shifting our mindset from what the culture offers to a biblical worldview allows us to parent with an eternal perspective, knowing that we are raising up world changers to influence the next generation.

Chapter 5

ROYALTY: UNDERSTANDING WHO WE ARE IN CHRIST

HER ROYAL HIGHNESS KATE MIDDLETON, Duchess of Cambridge, became royalty when she married Prince William. Kate was previously a commoner, not born into royalty herself; yet, today she carries herself with the dignity and elegance of a princess in the royal family. I am sure there was a learning curve on how to walk, talk, and dress like a princess, as well as how to act and perform duties like a princess. Some things, I'm sure, didn't just come naturally. I would think there was a lot to learn in her new role and her new way of life. While some of these practices may have been difficult and challenging at times, there was an expectation once she became part of the royal family. She had a new normal. Her life was no longer the same. Although being born a commoner will always be a part of her story, the expectations for her once she married into royalty define who she is today. Her way of thinking, her worldview, expectations, and challenges in life all changed.

You see, although Kate was born a common citizen, everything changed when she married Prince William. She is no longer defined as a commoner; she is defined as royalty. Now Kate, known as Catherine the Duchess of Cambridge, is royalty, and because of her status, the children she gives birth to are future heirs to the royal throne. The fruit of their marriage is royalty. Their children will inherit the blessings of royal throne and crown.

Although the first few months may have been a transition, Kate no longer wakes up questioning her place or status in England. She knows who she is. She knows whose she is. She belongs to Prince William and owns the fact that she belongs to the royal family. While her interactions, I am sure, are still very formal with Queen Elizabeth, she is family. Kate understands her role in the royal family. She carries herself with dignity and demonstrates not only a kindness and elegance, but also a confidence. She walks assuredly and with conviction in her role, understanding her place. She has direct access to the queen and all the dignitaries of England. She is the mother to the future king. Kate Middleton is royalty.

It was Father's Day 1978. It was a Sunday morning, and my family went to church that morning like we did every other Sunday. I still remember that my Sunday school teacher told us the story of Joseph and the coat of many colors. Following class, our family of four sat together, like always, in the front row pew, just right of center. I grew up at Highland Baptist Church in Waco, Texas, and every Sunday was the same: We attended Sunday school and then church together as a family. Our family was very well known at the church. We had a reputation as the Don Shipley family who sat in the front row every

Sunday—it was "our" pew. After church, we would go home, eat Sunday lunch, and then my parents took their Sunday afternoon nap.

But this Sunday was different; over lunch I told my parents that I wanted Jesus in my life. Although I don't remember the details, I do remember that I didn't have any questions. I was a six-year-old girl who was ready to say "yes" to Jesus. I understood very clearly that God sent His one and only Son, Jesus, to this sinful world and that He sacrificed His life by dying on the cross for my sin. I knew the Bible was true when it said, "For God so loved the world that he gave his one and only Son, that whoever believes in him shall not perish but have eternal life" (John 3:16). He loved me so much that He was willing to die and shed His blood so that I could be forgiven of my sins and live forever with Him one day in heaven. I understood that Jesus didn't stay dead. God miraculously raised Him from the dead three days later, and He is alive and at the right hand of God. I told my parents that I wanted to ask Jesus to be a part of my life.

I believe! "If you declare with your mouth, 'Jesus is Lord,' and believe in your heart that God raised him from the dead, you will be saved. For it is with your heart that you believe and are justified, and it is with your mouth that you profess your faith and are saved. As Scripture says, 'Anyone who believes in him will never be put to shame.' For there is no difference between Jew and Gentile—the same Lord is Lord of all and richly blesses all who call on him, for, 'Everyone who calls on the name of the Lord will be saved'" (Romans 10:9–13).

Now, I'm not sure if they were just tired or if they felt like I needed to make sure about this decision to follow Jesus since I was only six years old; but my parents told me to think about it while they went to take their Sunday afternoon nap. So, I went to my room, and I remember thinking that I knew, that I really knew, this is what I wanted—I wanted Jesus in my life. I knew that I was a sinner and that I needed a Savior. After my parents got in that Sunday afternoon nap, I went back and told them again, "I want to ask Jesus into my heart and life." My heart was sinful, and I needed Jesus to give me a clean heart and make me a part of His family. This time they sat down and made sure I understood what Jesus had done for me, and then the three of us knelt down beside my parents' bed and prayed, asking Jesus to be Lord and Savior of my life.

I love that I asked Jesus into my life on Father's Day because it is a beautiful reminder of what salvation represents. God the Father, maker of heaven and earth, adopts us into His family as sons and daughters when we give our lives to Him. He invites us into His royal family: "The Spirit himself testifies with our spirit that we are God's children. Now if we are children, then we are heirs—heirs of God and co-heirs with Christ" (Romans 8:16–17a).

The God of the universe, Almighty God, invites us into His family! That is a big deal! When we say yes to what God has done for us by giving His one and only Son to die for us, we not only have forgiveness of our sins by His shed blood, but we also have access to the Father and are made heirs. We become royalty. We become sons and daughters of the King of Kings and Lord of Lords. We are adopted into a kingdom that is more powerful than any other king or royalty. We are in the family of God. That means as sons and daughters of God, we are royalty just like Kate, Duchess of Cambridge, but we are even more royal because our Father is God!

I have been a daughter of the King of Kings for almost forty years! I am royalty because I am adopted into God's family. So Father's Day has a whole new meaning for me. On Father's Day, yes, I celebrate my earthly father who loves me very much, as well as my husband, the father of our three daughters; but I also celebrate that I am adopted into the kingdom of God. So for forty years, I have been a daughter of God, the ultimate King. I am His child. While one day I will die and leave this world, because I am a daughter of God, I will live forever in heaven with my Father God. There is no fear in death when we know where we are going. The party is just getting started!

When I can fully understand who I am in Christ, I will be able to better influence those around me and respond with a Christ-like attitude, knowing that I am imperfect but have been made perfect in Christ because of Jesus. I am a sinner in need of a Savior. I am changed. I am transformed in Christ. Kate Middleton became royalty. She is changed because she was chosen. She was given a new name. She is no longer a commoner. She commands respect simply because Prince William took her as his own. She dresses, behaves, and is expected to conduct herself as royalty so as to not tarnish the throne. She may not have been born into royalty, but she has accepted that she is a changed person. The same is true for us when we are adopted into the kingdom of God: We become royalty. God transforms us into His image. We become sons and daughters of the King of Kings and Lord of Lords. We have a higher place of royalty than even Kate Middleton!

When we become part of the kingdom of God, we too must understand who we are in Christ. We too must change the way we think, the way we act, the way we behave reflecting God's family. We can walk in confidence in knowing who we are in Christ. I am a daughter of the King! This confidence can be carried out in how we parent our children. When we can fully grasp who we are as a new creation, it will change our complete outlook on life and life's circumstances. We are changed. We are royalty. We have a new life. We have a new identity, a new name, because we are adopted into the family of God. We can walk in that confidence as we parent our children and live out our lives. We are not trying to parent like everyone else in the

> We have a high calling, a high standard for parenting, because of who and whose we are in Christ.

world, because the world is not our family or our identity. We won't look like everyone else. Just as Kate Middleton doesn't look like or live like everyone else, we too should look different from the world we live in because of who we are in Christ. We are no longer a part of this world. This is not our home. We have been adopted into the family of God. We can walk in that confidence, knowing our identity as part of God's royal family. We have a high calling, a high standard for parenting, because of who and whose we are in Christ.

Just as Mary was chosen and called to be the mother of Jesus, we are chosen and called to be the mother of the children God has placed in our care. We should embrace that job as the greatest and highest calling we have been given. It is an opportunity, a gift, and an honor to be chosen to influence and parent the gifts we have been given. We will look different from the world because we are no longer a part of this world. Our inheritance is in heaven, not in this world. We must get to the place that we are not swayed by what others think because we are confident of who we are in Christ.

We aren't looking to parent with each new fad or searching for an easy fix. We are not looking for culture to give us the latest remedy or the newest parenting tips for success. The world and culture are not our measuring stick. We are not looking to our peers, we are looking to our Father, God Almighty, as our source for wisdom. Once we fully understand who we are and whose we are, we won't even care about impressing those around us. We won't be caught up in the comparison game. We won't be driven by fear. We will no longer live our lives in insecurity, but rather a confidence in the authority that comes with being the sons and daughters of the King.

As a daughter of God Almighty, God is my authority. Oprah is not my authority. Dr. Phil is not my authority. God is my authority. Facebook is not my standard. Moms in my playgroup are not my standard. Moms from my kid's school are not my standard. Moms from church are not my standard. When we are looking for approval from anyone other than God, we are not fully living with confidence in who we are in Christ. "Am I now trying to win the approval of human beings, or of God? Or am I trying to please people? If I were still trying to please people, I would not be a servant of Christ" (Galatians 1:10). God is my standard. God is the only perfect parent. So why compare or set the bar with anyone but the best? Why would I look to what other sinful imperfect people are doing, when I can look to the Creator of life and the ultimate authority and King? God, my Father, created the universe and spoke the world into existence, so why would I look to anyone but Him for wisdom when it comes to parenting the children He entrusted to me? In fact, I will give an account one day, not to Facebook, not to our neighbors, not to our family—I will give an account to the Almighty God. It is His approval

I should seek, not my mom groups, PTA moms, swim moms, or soccer moms. I should not even seek approval from my church groups. The only approval I need is my Father's—my Heavenly Father.

Motherhood is a high calling, and when we understand who we are in Christ, as daughters of the King of Kings, God Himself, we can walk in a confidence and security in our identity being found in Him and not in our parenting. Our children are not here to satisfy us or give us a name or identity. Motherhood is not my identity. My career is not my identity. My home or the car I drive is not my identity. My identity is in Christ, and in Christ alone. Suddenly, the insecurity and fear we were paralyzed by before when comparing ourselves and our mothering to others is gone! Understanding who we are in Christ gives an entirely new meaning to motherhood and the confidence we can have as a mother. I am now able to cheer for you as a fellow mother because I am no longer in competition against you. I understand who I am in Christ, and because my identity is in Christ alone, I am not competing with fellow moms.

Once we can understand that our value and worth as a woman can be found only in Christ, we will never find satisfaction trying to measure up to others. And if we are living vicariously through our children, we are putting undo pressure on them to succeed and are looking for them to bring us joy and satisfaction instead of our status being found in Christ. When we understand who we are in Jesus, we will be able to put on the blinders to what is around us (Facebook, Pinterest, other families' successes, vacations, careers), and we will be able to focus on what Christ has called us to do within our own family. I will then be able to stay in my own lane as I run my race, and I can cheer for you as you run your race. Fellow mothers, let's learn how to cheer for one another instead of tearing one another apart. Our envy and ravenous desire to destroy one another only reveals a heart that is not found in Jesus and an insecurity in not understanding who we are in Christ.

When we give our lives to Jesus and we come into His family, we are given a new name. We are adopted into the family of God. Just like Kate Middleton was given a new name, a new title, a new home, and a new life, I was changed at six years of age when I was adopted in the family of God. I can walk in confidence, knowing that I am His child. I have access to the Father God Almighty because I am a daughter of the King of Kings. I have authority in the name of Jesus because of whose I am. There is power in the name of Jesus, and I have access to that authority because of the authority I am given as a daughter of the King. I can parent out of this confidence and raise my three daughters to come to know their need for Jesus, making them aware of the access that they too can have in their Father God. As our children have come to know Jesus as their personal Lord and Savior, our home is powerful. Our home is royalty. Our home is sacred. My children are His, and we can walk in the blessing of living life with a confidence of who we are in Christ.

As mothers, when we can parent from this place of confidence, we give our children the opportunity to begin to see life from an eternal perspective. Just as little Prince George and Princess Charlotte will see life from a different worldview than the commoner in England, our children have the opportunity to see life as royalty in Christ with a biblical worldview when we parent from that perspective.

Instead of our homes being filled with envy, fear, pride, and comparison, our homes can be filled with the fruit of the Spirit: love, joy, peace, patience, kindness, goodness, faithfulness, gentleness, and self-control (Galatians 5:22–23a). Motherhood is an opportunity to create royal homes across the globe, places for the Spirit of God to dwell. Our actions and attitudes can reflect this as we live out the gospel and share the redemptive story to the lost and dying world around us.

When we understand who we are in Christ, this revolutionizes our identity and role as mothers. We begin to parent with an eternal perspective. We begin to stay focused on our goal for parenting. We develop a game plan for suc-

> Motherhood is an opportunity to create royal homes across the globe, places for the Spirit of God to dwell.

cess. We understand who we are, which frees us from the bondage of fear and comparison to our fellow mothers. We learn how to stay in our own lane. We begin to understand the authority and power we have in the name of Jesus and walk in that confidence of who we are in Christ. We understand that we are royalty and this is not our home. Motherhood becomes a precious responsibility and an opportunity to invest in the kingdom of heaven. When we begin living life as royalty, our identity changes. Our worldview shifts. Our identity in Christ defines who and whose we are. We begin focusing on raising up disciples and world changers.

Chapter 6

ETERNAL PERSPECTIVE

YOU COULD BARELY FIND A parking space in the large church parking lot. The church was packed, filled with families of school-aged children who were missing school that day to mourn the loss of a fellow student. A varsity volleyball player, well-liked by everyone she met, was gone. A freak accident of nature left a huge impact and emptiness among an entire community. Our family filed in to find a seat toward the back of the large church auditorium. One of the largest churches in the community was filled to capacity. A somber mood filled the air. No one should have to lose a child. No one should have to say good-bye to a brother or sister when they are still just kids. It was only weeks before that we were all laughing and enjoying life together. How is a mom ever supposed to get over the loss of a beloved daughter? Why should a mom have to, in one moment, bring life into the world and in another moment lay that same life to rest, buried deep in the ground, marked only by a name and date? How does a mom ever recover from this kind of tragedy? The pain sometimes feels so suffocating that the sheer idea of getting out of bed is all one can do to live another day without a child gone too soon.

While still painful, we prepare ourselves to say good-bye to the elderly. We know their time has come, and while they will be missed, it's the circle of life that is natural and expected. But the pain of saying good-bye to a child is not what is expected or natural in life. Several years ago, my husband and I went to the funeral home to support our friends, Philip and Lisa, who had lost their baby girl. When we walked into the dimly lit room set aside for the family, there was a small casket on top of a table. The little box was no more than a foot long. A precious baby girl, Adeline, lay inside. What do you say? How do you respond? It feels like anything you say is wrong. It seems there are no appropriate words in a time of sorrow and grief of this magnitude. In my heart all I wanted to do was to comfort or somehow make it better, but there was nothing that I could say or do but just stand there and let them know we were there. I thought about what I would do if I were the weeping mother who had just lost one of my three daughters. How would I respond? Would I be angry? Would I be grateful for the short time I had been given? Would I have regrets? Would I be reliving everything that I would have changed? Would I have stayed up a little bit longer to hold my daughter as she fell asleep that night? Would I have put down my phone long enough to let her know she is all that matters to me?

Like any parent, I think the hardest thing we could face would be the loss of a child. I really can't imagine there being any other pain so tragic and so hard than to know that in a moment's notice you are holding life and in the next moment burying the life you had conceived and brought into this world. But none of us are promised another day. This lack of promise for another day of life, another breath, creates in us an urgency to embrace today. This shouldn't spark fear or incite us to parent from a place of fear, but rather should encourage us to live our lives with intention and purpose and passion.

It was just another crisp fall morning when I woke up, or so I thought. Reagan, our firstborn, was just five months old. We had slept in and had just woken up around 8:30 AM that morning. Todd had left for work and already was in downtown D.C. at a congressional hearing in the Capitol. I was a stay-at-home mom at this point in time. Like any other morning when Reagan woke up, I changed her diaper and headed into the family room to nurse her in our small townhome in Springfield, Virginia. I had turned on the TV to watch the Today Show with Katie Couric and Matt Lauer, and by the time I sat down, Matt was in the middle of reporting that one of the World Trade Center towers in New York City had just been hit by a plane. It was unexplained as to whether it was an accident or not, but within minutes, the second tower was hit. It was September 11, 2001.

As history now explains, shortly after the two planes hit the Twin Towers in New York, a plane hit the side of the Pentagon and another plane that was headed to Washington, D.C., was diverted and crashed in a field in Pennsylvania. When the planes hit New York, reports began coming in that the White House and Capitol were being evacuated. At the time, I had no idea that my husband was in the Capitol. I knew he was downtown, but I did not learn of his location until later. Panicked, I began trying to call Todd at work, knowing that his office was in between the White House and the Capitol. I was unable to reach him. All of the phone lines were jammed. There was so much unknown. Life as we knew it had suddenly changed.

Finally, I was able to reach someone in his office who let me know that they had been able to reach him and that he had been evacuated from the Capitol and was trying to leave the city. For the next three to four hours, Todd and some of his colleagues were just trying to cross one of the bridges to get out of the city and into Virginia. It was complete gridlock. I don't even remember him coming home that day. Everything became a blur. The Capitol police officers who had come into the congressional hearing he was attending had whispered into the congressman's ear. His gavel came down with authority, and the congressman declared that the hearing was postponed and that the Capitol needed to be evacuated. No one really knew what was happening so it was kind of like when the fire alarms go off in a restaurant and everyone looks around to figure out what to do but no one runs. As employees were leaving the building, the police officers were yelling, "RUN! Get away from the Capitol!" Obviously, Todd, like everyone else in D.C., did not return to work for the next several days. We visited the Pentagon and saw the ashes that filled the huge gaping hole where the third plane had hit. This was our generation's introduction to war.

A couple years ago, Todd and I visited the site in Pennsylvania where the plane crashed that we later learned had been meant to hit the U.S. Capitol. The brave passengers who were on Flight 93 that day became even more real to us as we looked out into that empty field, now a memorial. Reading their names that were etched into the stone memorial brought back floods of memories from that morning on September 11th. We stood there, frozen in silence, as we realized the passengers on that plane may have died in place of my husband. I could have been a widow with a newborn that day. The two of us had a completely fresh and new appreciation for the passengers like Todd Beamer who said, "Let's roll," and fought back against the hijackers and saved hundreds or thousands of lives in the process.

Life is a roller coaster, and there are twists and turns that we just can't prepare for. A few years ago, our family of five was traveling on I-95 headed south to spend the week in Myrtle Beach for spring break. As we were making our way down the interstate, we noticed that the weather was getting worse by the hour. We were passing through North Carolina and turned on the radio to find out that there were tornados spotted in the area. After stopping to get something to eat and fill up our SUV with gas, we had been back on the road for about an hour. The rain had picked up, and the traffic had slowed down almost to a stop. Cars were stopping under the underpasses to wait for the storm to pass. We came up to a complete stop where all lanes were backed up on both sides of the interstate.

Within about two minutes of our coming to a complete stop, we looked up, and to the left of us, we saw the funnel. There was nowhere to go. There was nowhere to hide. We, like many others, were completely exposed, sitting in our cars on the interstate, and we watched in awe as the tornado funnel moved directly in our path as it made its way across the interstate. Our girls were in the backseat of the car. It all happened so fast. We began to feel our black SUV shake. I had been driving. I gripped the steering wheel. With my mind racing, I tried to figure out what would happen to the five of us if the car flipped or if we got picked up and thrown with the power of the funnel. As I gripped the steering wheel with fear and panic, I prayed out loud, "Protect us, Lord Jesus. Protect us, Lord Jesus." I just kept repeating that simple prayer out loud as we felt the tornado sweep across our SUV, shaking it as the funnel went directly over our car.

The funnel was now ripping a large billboard sign right off of the metal poles, throwing the sign into the air, mangled and torn. We looked at each other, not believing that an actual tornado had just passed over our car, shaking it with violent power and doing damage as it moved across the highway. By this point, all I could muster was to repeat, "Thank you, Jesus! Thank you, Jesus!" All five of us were okay. Our car didn't have a scratch on it. We had not flipped. We felt the power of the tornado, and we were in the middle of the storm, but we were safe. God had His hand of protection over us.

After the storm passed, everyone around us got out of their cars to survey the damage. We were the lucky ones. Just a few cars ahead of ours, a huge eighteen-wheeler had been flipped on its side, large billboard signs were ripped off of poles, cars had been shifted from their positions, and huge trees were uprooted and thrown across the interstate. We were unable to leave or move for hours. It was close to nightfall before they could get in enough emergency crews to move the eighteen-wheeler that was flipped and spread across the interstate. Emergency crews had to come in with chainsaws to cut up the trees that were lying across the middle of the roadway and blocking passage. I am not aware of anyone hurt, but there were hours of walking around the interstate, surveying all the damage with hearts full of gratitude that we had all survived. We were grateful to be alive. We had lived to tell about the tornado that went directly over our car. I will never forget the feeling of our car shaking in that frightful moment and having no clue how to protect our children. We were not in control. But God was in control! Life is short. None of us are in control—only God.

I am not promised a long life, and neither are my girls. My husband could have died on 9/11. We all could have died in the tornado. Life is short on this earth. Eternity is lasting and forever! Even if I live to be 100 (I hope I am still dancing at 100), life is so short compared to eternity.

Most kids will leave home around age eighteen. While we still have influence in our children's lives after they leave home and begin on their own, the fact that we only have face-to-face daily influence on a child's life for eighteen years is absolutely sobering! Talk about a short amount of time. I have only a couple years left with my oldest still at home.

We enter into motherhood loving the "idea" of being a mother. You dream of taking your little ones to the park, going to the mall shopping together, attending their baseball games, taking them camping, teaching them how to fish or ride a bike, taking them to their first professional sports game, and the list goes on. We dream of the perfect childhood for them. We want to give them a better life than we had. Nothing is wrong with this! Of course, we want to give our children a fabulous childhood. We want to make memories and cherish every moment of being a mother.

If you have ever talked to a new mom, she will often tell you she can't see past diapers and nursing every three hours. Her life is on repeat. She barely has time to take a shower, and a nap is a luxury. Having any time alone, including going to the bathroom alone, is a gift felt straight from heaven. Motherhood can be exhausting. It can be lonely. It can be draining and hard. By the time you take your child to preschool, those three hours are suddenly filled with mundane responsibilities like grocery shopping and are rarely filled with any lavish luxury other than a few moments of alone time. In my years of working with the mothers of preschoolers, I often encourage moms not to lose sight of the fact that these hard years go by way too fast. While a mother may feel like her life of diapers and nursing babies will never end, the reality is it ends far too soon!

If you choose to send your child to school outside the home, it is at this moment, normally around age five or six, that you are passing the baton and giving someone else the power of influence and time with your child. That means that you have five short years of having your child at home, completely to yourself, and that is if you don't do any kind of daycare or preschool before kindergarten. And by the time your children begin school, they end up spending more time there than at home with you. If you do the math, this means that from the time they wake up, go to school, attend extracurricular activities, come home, and go to bed, you as the mom have fewer hours in the day with your child than others do.

The days become longer and longer as your child begins to spend more time outside the home in school, on the ball field, and with friends. The teacher has more hours in the day with your little person than you do. This is sobering! So not only do we have eighteen short years with them living under our roof, we also are sharing our time with them for a large majority of those years. This is why it is critical to know who our children are spending time with, knowing who their teachers are, what school they are going to, the influence of coaches and teams, and who their friends are. All of these things matter because if I as the mom have only a small percentage of the day influencing my child's worldview, I need to make certain that I'm choosing the right kinds of places and persons that will be sharing in this very important role. Influence matters.

It is crucial that not only am I being intentional in giving my child a solid foundation and Christ-centered biblical worldview so he or she can stand firm, but that I am also being intentional in how I'm spending the eighteen years I am given with them under my care. I have been entrusted with the care and upbringing of these lives, so how I use my time matters. Counting the number of hours in the day that I have with my preschooler verses the number of hours I have with them once they are school-aged reinforces the high calling of motherhood. This also validates and reinforces to moms of preschoolers that the time you have with your children before they go off to school is vital. It is in those first five years that you are establishing the framework for their worldview. You are setting the foundation for parenting from an eternal perspective.

For those of you who have small children and are in the early years of parenting, understanding that the foundational years are paramount is key. Let's imagine that you are building a new home for your family. You have purchased the land. You are beyond excited about creating your dream home. The architect has drawn up plans. You are picking out cabinets, curtains, flooring, granite, the works. It is your dream home! As the foundation is being poured, the weather turns for the worst as a storm hits. Once it passes, you can see that, although the foundation was poured, there are obvious places in the structure where there are gaps. Debris from the storm has settled in the foundation, and overall the foundation needs repair. There were some pretty significant oversights. In your excitement and enthusiasm for your dream home, you willingly overlook the sloppy foundation and move forward with all the fun stuff—the things that people will notice. After all, no one actually sees the foundation. That is hidden. That is underneath the surface and is not what people see when they come over for dinner. What people see is the fun stuff like the dark hardwood floors, the Pottery Barn furniture, the granite countertops, the chairs you found at Home Goods, the impeccable cabinets with the to-die-for backsplash! This is what people see, so this is what matters. No one sees the foundation, so we can just hope that we don't have problems with the foundation down the road.

The problem here, of course, is the foundation is paramount. It is critical. It is the crux for the entire home. Yes, the granite and window treatments are important, and they make a house look like an inviting home, but if we miss the importance of the foundation, our beautiful home can crumble. The foundation is what holds the home together. What happens when that next storm comes? If the foundation is not secure, the house can have damage or even be so structurally unsound that it is in a constant state of risk. Maybe there are faults in the foundation that cause shifting, leading to cracks moving up the walls.

Moms, follow me. Our parenting is a lot like these homes. We can look really amazing and fabulous to our girlfriends and the other moms at school, but if our foundation is shaky, we risk disaster. We can be so bent on striving for the "decor" and window treatments—for our kids to look fabulous from the outside—that we risk destruction. We make sure that our kids are attending all of the social activities, are on the best teams, and are involved in the youth group, but that is all external. They may be into all the sports, captain of the team, student body president, leading full and busy lives running from school to ballet or soccer, and yet if their foundation is not solid, they are at risk.

Our culture has become bent on who can be busier, who has the best Pinterest parties, whose kids are in the most activities, and who got into what preschool. We have become a generation of moms who are more concerned about our appearance and "window treatments" than with securing our foundation. Our priorities are out of balance. When we don't prioritize the importance of a secure and solid foundation, we will always put our children at risk. The foundation years are so important. They are critical. They cannot be overlooked or ignored. Building a solid foundation takes time. It can't be rushed or thrown together. The foundation is when we teach our children the basics. They don't just come into this world knowing respect, right from wrong, or having a giving and caring heart. No, our children come into this world with a "MINE" mentality of selfishness, pride, and envy. Our children come into this world as sinners. They may be cute and adorable, but they are sinners in need of a Savior.

Unfortunately, we are as guilty as our society for feeding this entitlement mentality. We encourage our children to have a heart of sin when they think they deserve and are entitled to success and no failure in life. We are only growing their already innate sin nature. We are feeding what must be starved. Our job as moms is to be willing to do the hard work. The hard work means showing our children their sin. We must come alongside our children and help them understand they are not the center of the universe. We must help them move away from a self-centered mentality to a servant's heart of caring for those around them.

This is where the foundation is critical. What are we teaching our children at two years of age? Are we teaching them that they don't have to share? Because, of course, that is your toy, or even if it's not your toy, you want it and we get what we want in life. Or when your child is three or four, do they look at you with defiance in their eyes and willfully say "no" to you? Let's face it, even if your child can't walk yet, you still have opportunities to teach them. If you tell your nine-month-old, who is crawling, not to touch the light socket and she laughs and touches it anyway, it's not cute or something to be encouraged. This is where the foundation work begins. If, when you call your child to come to you and, instead, his cute little eighteen-month-old face smiles as he runs the other way to be chased, then you have some foundation work to be done. Moms, your authority as a parent is not a joke. It is not something to take lightly. The first five years of parenting are paramount and critical for laying the foundation. In order to parent with eternal perspective, we must realize our days are short. "Teach us to number our days, that we may gain a heart of wisdom," the psalmist says in Psalm 90:12.

Let's look at our days from an eternal perspective. If I have, at most, one hundred years on this earth, but during only eighteen of those one hundred years my child is living with me at home under my authority, then I have a very small window of influence. Now let's look at those years of ages six through eighteen when they are at school. Those years become shared, partnership years. These are the years that you are sharing your children with the school, their teachers, the church, youth group, friends, and sports teams. That leaves you with approximately five dedicated years of 1:1 time to build a firm foundation before you begin to have real outside influences alongside your parenting. This is absolutely daunting! While I am very intentional in my choice of schooling, teachers, friends, and sports, I can't control all of these influences. As they get older, I want those experiences to become more varied; I want them to be exposed so they are more prepared to face the world and culture with a solid biblical worldview.

Moms of school-aged children or even teenagers, do not panic! Hope is not lost. Do not become discouraged and let fear rule your heart. While you may be questioning how you can redeem what is lost, realizing that you quite possibly were not intentional in those foundational years, do not fear that it is too late. God is such a good God. He is a loving Father who always meets us right where we are. "If any of you lacks wisdom, you should ask God, who gives generously to all without finding fault, and it will be given to you" (James 1:5). God freely and generously gives us wisdom when we ask! But we MUST ask. It doesn't mean it will be easy. There may, in fact, be a lot of repair work to be done. But when we ask God for wisdom, He promises to meet us where we are and give us what we need. So while the foundational years may have passed you by, ask God how to navigate where you are today to begin the process of being intentional in reaching your child's heart.

While I hope to have influence long after eighteen years, those years that my child is at home are only a blink of an eye compared to eternity. This reality is not a scare tactic. This is simply a reality check to put our parenting into perspective for all of eternity. Eternity is forever. Our spirits will live forever. I want my children to spend eternity with Jesus; therefore, I want to use my time wisely to build a lasting foundation that frames their adulthood. I want to be purposeful in teaching my children about God's love for them. I want them to know that His love, grace, forgiveness, and redemption are real. I want them to know Jesus and have their own personal experience of who He is. I want to help shape and mold my children into the likeness of Christ. I want God to teach me how to number my days so that I have His wisdom in seeing life with an eternal perspective. Our jobs as mothers truly can impact eternity.

It is not the church's job to raise our children spiritually. While the church absolutely should support the role of the family in raising up a godly generation, we cannot shirk our responsibilities in the home. We can't expect that taking our children to church for one hour a week will be sufficient or do the job. Rather, the church should, instead, be a complement to what I am already doing at home. Oftentimes, we expect the church to do our job, providing our children's spiritual training for us because we are too lazy or intimidated to do it ourselves at home.

We must know the Word of God so that we can teach the Word of God to our children. We have to stop passing the buck and accept responsibility. God has given authority to the parents to be the primary influencers of our children. As parents, God has called us to train our children. That authority is mine, not the education system's, not the government's. It is not the job of the church to reach my child's heart for Christ. That is my training ground as the parent. Instead, the church should be a weekly support system that reinforces what I am instilling at home. Their job is to come alongside me as the parent. We should be in a partnership. We should collaborate in working

> We have to stop passing the buck and accept responsibility. God has given authority to the parents to be the primary influencers of our children.

together, but the responsibility falls on us as parents.

Moms and dads, we have a calling and a responsibility to reach our child's heart for Christ. We are being lazy, and even disobedient, when we want to give that job to the church instead of owning the responsibility that God has given to us. We must stop passing the job off to others. It is our job as moms and dads to teach our children about Jesus. Churches, youth groups, and Christian schools are to partner with us—not parent our child. Parents must heed the wake-up call to take ownership of this responsibility that God has entrusted to us. God has designated that authority to the parents. Mothers, we are called. We are chosen! Motherhood has eternal significance.

As parents, we are instructed to teach our children 24/7. God charged parents with the responsibility of being at a constant place of conversation and instruction with their children. This was with the purpose of parents continuously reminding their children of who God is, His laws and His faithfulness. There should never be a generation that is not reminded of God's faithfulness. He is a good Father. It should be a constant conversation. "Love the Lord your God with all your heart and with all your soul and with all your strength. These commandments that I give you today are to be on your hearts. Impress them on your children. Talk about them when you sit at home and when you walk along the road, when you lie down and when you get up. Tie them as symbols on your hands and bind them on your foreheads. Write them on the doorframes of your houses and on your gates" (Deuteronomy 6:5–9). We too are called to teach and instruct our children of God's principles for how we too must live. "What does the Bible say?" should be a constant conversation in our homes. This starts early from the time we take our children on a walk and we remind them that God is the Creator of everything they see and enjoy (Genesis 1). It continues as we have deeper discussions with our teens about their worldview.

Communication with our children is on-going. Many times we forfeit opportunities to engage in conversation with our teens, and yet this is a critical stage that we must not let the conversation end. Whether it is in the foundational years or the teen years, we must point our children to Jesus. When we wake up, we share with them the promises of God and that today is a fresh day filled with God's mercy (Lamentations 3:22–23). Over dinner, we ask them about their day and use those opportunities to teach godly principles for living. As we tuck them in at night, cherish those tender moments of talking to God together. "Fix these words of mine in your hearts and minds. . . . Teach them to your children, talking about them when you sit at home and when you walk along the road, when you lie down and when you get up" (Deuteronomy 11:18–19). Our opportunities to teach our children are endless. God is instructing us as parents to be in a constant place of sharing the gospel with our children at all times. It should be in the forefront of our minds and hearts and a continual and constant on-going conversation.

When we choose to pass this commission onto someone else, we are giving up the authority and privilege that rightfully belongs to us as parents. We may take our children to church with the assumption that it is the church's rightful job to teach our children about God. Or we may enroll our children in a Christian school and then task them with responsibility of reaching our children's hearts. Oftentimes this occurs because we don't know the Bible well enough to teach it ourselves. We are not living out the gospel in our homes; we are not instructing our children 24/7.

If I send my child to church each week to attend youth group or Sunday school or send them to church camp, then I feel better because someone else is impacting their lives. This is not what the Bible teaches! The Bible has given this authority of instruction to the parents! It's the mother and father who should be picking up the mantle of authority with honor and pride, humbled by the responsibility. We have been tasked with this great privilege. And yet, more often than not, we don't want the job. Or we don't feel equipped to do the job. We feel too insecure in our own relationship with Jesus to be able to talk about it and teach it well. We have bought into the lie that Satan wants us to believe—that our relationship with the Lord is personal and private.

As parents, we have been blessed with the responsibility to teach our children about Jesus, and we need to be fully ready ourselves in order to be up to the challenge. We need to step up our game. It is not a Christian school's job. It is not the church's job. God has given the family, the mother and father, the authority and the responsibility. It is my job as a mother.

We live in a lost and dying world. Even after death, we will live forever, either with our Father God in heaven or eternally separated from Him in hell. That thought scares me. That is sobering. My greatest goal as a mother is to reach my children's hearts for Jesus. I want them to know Him personally. I want them to spend eternity with Him in heaven. It is that kind of parenting with an eternal perspective that changes everything. Suddenly, status no longer matters, popularity is not important, the only thing that is left is knowing what happens when we die. The one hundred years we may get on this earth are only a second compared to eternity. The eighteen short years we get to parent our children under our roof is even shorter. Those years go by so fast. And to think that we have only five years to be with them 24/7 before we begin to share them with the school is even more sobering. Life is short, really short. We are not promised tomorrow. While we do not need to live in fear or parent from a place of fear, we must be intentional in understanding our opportunity and potential for influence. I have a very short window in the big picture, but my reach has eternal significance.

Chapter 7

INTENTIONAL PARENTING

JANUARY 20, 2009, was a bitterly cold day in Washington, D.C. On the steps of the nation's Capitol, Barack Obama was being sworn in as our new president. President George W. Bush had served our country for eight years and was leaving office. There is pomp and circumstance as the changing of power occurs. Across the Potomac River, a large crowd had gathered inside an airport hangar at Andrews Air Force Base. The once-empty hangar was now packed as a crowd gathered around a roped-off, make-shift stage and waited for President Bush to arrive and take his final flight home on Air Force One. The crowd was primarily made up of the staff and political appointees who had worked for President Bush. We were in attendance with our three princesses, Reagan, Jordan, and Riley. All three girls were covered in many layers to weather the bitterly cold January morning, but as people began to pack in, the body heat of the crowd kept us all a little too warm. I began to worry that the girls would over-heat, unable to move in the tight quarters. You couldn't turn or move. We just stood still and in place, packed in like sardines, holding our coveted spot in the hopes of one last view of the president. Gratefully, our family had arrived early and were right along the rope line. The girls were in matching red coats with big red bows in their hair. We stood in place for several hours before the ceremony across town had even begun. Finally, some TVs hung inside the hangar began showing that the official ceremony had begun.

President Bush and soon-to-be-sworn-in President Obama were in black overcoats surrounded by their families. Congressmen filled the chairs around them on the steps of the Capitol overlooking the National Mall crowded with spectators. As the ceremony came to a close and President Obama was sworn in as the new president, he and Michelle along with their girls headed to the presidential motorcade to make their way down Pennsylvania Avenue to their new home, the White House. At the same time, President Bush, Laura, and their girls, as well as Vice President Dick Cheney and Lynne Cheney, were headed across the Potomac River in Marine One to the hangar at Andrews Air Force Base for their final departure.

Just outside the hangar, Air Force One was sitting on the runway in all her majesty. There were a few parting words. President George W. Bush thanked his faithful staff and appointees and said his good-byes. After he spoke, he and Laura walked the rope line to shake hands, stopping for an occasional photograph before making their way to board Air Force One. He and Laura both came by and stopped and said a few words to our family. He patted the top of my husband's bald head and gave me a kiss on the cheek. I leaned in to tell him thank you for his service, and then we took a family photo with him.

Years earlier, President Bush had held our oldest daughter, Reagan, on her first birthday on the White House lawn at the annual White

House Easter Egg Roll. Now, seven years later, we were a family of five taking a picture with him. It is a memory I will never forget. To watch history being made right before your eyes is surreal. Gracious and humble as always, President Bush and Laura walked in between two rows of military men and women that lined the path to the stairs of that majestic aircraft. The couple walked the long and steep stairs of the plane, stood at the top, turned and waved a final wave and salute, and then took their places inside for one final flight aboard Air Force One. There was a new commander in chief, and the Bushes were off to their home in Texas. We watched the long blue and white plane with the presidential seal taxi the runway and ascend into the cold blue sky.

That day began a long journey for our family, as there were a lot of changes in D.C., including the economic crisis that hit the nation. The housing market declined, people were looking for jobs, and times were challenging. My husband, Todd, was one of hundreds in transition now looking for a job. Every president appoints his own staff, not only internally at the White House but also throughout the entire federal government. So with every outgoing president, hundreds of people lose their jobs, while the incoming president brings in his own team and appointments. So, we knew he'd be looking for a new job after January 20th, we just didn't expect the economic state of the nation to make it such a hard transition.

Our family made a lot of personal adjustments as we experienced our own personal financial crisis in between jobs. The next three years would be challenging, to say the least, for our family. It was what I refer to as our "desert experience." I often felt like I was identifying with the children of Israel wandering around in the desert. I was just hoping that our experience wouldn't last for forty years like their wilderness experience had. Trusting that God would provide was a new kind of learning curve for us all. We were experiencing our own personal faith being put to the test when we had to really come to grips with the questions: Do I trust God in the hard times? Is God good all the time? While we had a lot of questions and concerns, our faith never wavered. Our foundation was secure, knowing that God was faithful. But that doesn't mean that it wasn't hard. It was very hard! We weren't sure how God would provide, but we were confident He would.

God did provide; it just took much longer than we anticipated. But God showed up for us in that journey in ways that we never could have imagined. We received anonymous gift cards in the mail that were constant reminders that He loved us and that we weren't forgotten. He was providing in unique ways, just not the ways we would have mapped or planned for ourselves. It was during those lean years, while things were hard, that our faith increased rather than decreased. We became more reliant on God in this trial and testing period in our lives because that is the only place we could put our trust. There were no other options. I like to think of it as going through the fire for refinement. We were being refined and purified for what was next, although we had no idea what "next" looked like.

This desert journey, or refinement, challenged the way we parented. Our faith was tested, which naturally extends into how we talk to our children and parent them in a hard journey. It was a new learning curve for me as a mother to trust God, and I was able to pass that on to our girls. We found a new place of contentment and gratitude, not in external material things, but in a quiet place of solitude with Jesus.

On January 21, 2009, the day after President Bush left office, we were all at home, because my husband no longer had a job. That evening before the girls were heading to bed, our youngest daughter, Riley, unbeknownst to us, had gone to our middle daughter, Jordan's room, to inform her that she wanted to become a Christian and ask Jesus to be in her life. She was three and a half years old.

Riley likes things on her own terms. She reminds me a lot of myself! We had actively been talking to her about Jesus, but we weren't pushing anything. We were just telling Riley, as we did with all of our girls, that Jesus loves her, died for her sins, and wants to have a personal relationship with her. Riley had never shown any real interest in praying to ask Jesus to be in her life. She would listen intently as we would read Bible stories, but then she would be ready to go play. We knew our job was to be consistent in helping our girls understand their need for Christ, but the Holy Spirit would have to convict them of their need for Him. So we planted seeds.

That cold January evening, Riley had gotten out of bed, walked into her sister's bedroom, and told Jordan that she wanted Jesus in her life. Jordan, five at the time, came to get us and report this great news. Our entire family ended up in Jordan's room, where Riley was waiting for Jordan to return. We proceeded to ask Riley about this great news that she had told Jordan. Riley, a confident three-year-old, looked us in the eyes and boldly said, "I want Jesus in my life." She was ready to ask Jesus to forgive her of her sins, and she wanted Him to be a part of her life. We were ecstatic!

At this point, all three of our girls had now asked Jesus to be in their lives and were making their need for Jesus personal. It was no longer just us talking to them, it was now personal for them. Each one of our princesses had their own personal relationship with Jesus. The Holy Spirit was moving in our family big time. I believe the timing of Riley asking Jesus into her life, the day after Todd began looking for a new job, was not a coincidence. It was the Holy Spirit preparing all five of us individually, and as a family, to be ready for all of the changes, challenges, and new adventures that He was about to take us on.

That evening the five of us prayed with Riley. Then, Riley herself prayed, asking Jesus to come into her little life, to forgive her of her sins, and to live with her forever. She was committing her life to Jesus. New life began. Spiritual birth had occurred. We sang "Happy Birthday," taking pictures and videos to mark the special and monumental night! After hugs and kisses, the girls all went to sleep.

Our time in the "desert" was really one of the greatest experiences I believe our family has had in our parenting journey. It is hard to imagine that one of the most difficult times you go through as a couple or as a family can actually end up being one of the best times of your life. Although hard and extremely challenging (to the point that sometimes we were rationing the basics of bread and milk), the opportunities we had in teaching our children to trust God, no matter what, were invaluable. You can't put a price tag on life experiences. When you go through really hard times, you either run from God or to Him. Your faith either grows or you have no faith or foundation to stand on. You either turn to fear and worry, or you become so confident in who you are as a child of God that nothing will shake your faith.

I think one of the greatest lessons our daughters learned in those three years was that they saw firsthand that we could trust God no

> When you go through really hard times, you either run from God or to Him.

matter what. We saw God provide in unique ways. There were times we would go out to the mailbox, and inside we would find anonymous gift cards. We were seeing God provide for our basic needs in a real and tangible way, and our faith increased. Our family mantra was to count out loud and yell, "One. Two. Three. God rocks!" When God provided, we were quick to thank Him as a family. We knew that those gifts ultimately came from God. He was providing for us and using others to bless our family. I had a very wise girlfriend encourage me to begin keeping a "Gratefulness Journal" and write down every single way that God provided, whether it was hand-me-down clothes, gift cards, someone buying me a Starbucks drink, or someone dropping off groceries. As we kept account of God's faithfulness in this journal, we began to see that God was providing for every need in ways that we never could have imagined. During a time of extreme pain and questions, we were grateful.

One afternoon, I had gone out to the mailbox to get the mail for the day. I was flipping through the stack and noticed a white envelope with no return label. Todd wasn't at home at the time. The girls were upstairs. I tore open the envelope to find a card that had scripted across the front, "My God will supply all of my needs." Inside, the card was blank. No note—nothing—except two $100 gift cards. You have to understand this was like gold! I felt like we had just won the lottery! I ran upstairs as fast as I could to excitedly tell the girls what I had just opened. Smiles spread across their faces as wide as the Grand Canyon. I simply asked them, "What should we do?" In my heart and head, I was thinking that we should say a prayer thanking God for this amazing gift, but I waited for their response before encouraging them to give thanks with me. Immediately, without skipping a beat, Jordan, our middle daughter, said with confidence, "We should pray blessings on the person who sent them." My heart melted. They got it! My daughters understood and got it! They weren't concerned about how we would spend the money. They immediately knew it was a gift from their Father God in heaven. God had used someone to bless us, and our girls wanted to pray for that person to be blessed in return for their generosity and kindness.

We haven't done it all right. But these are the types of lessons that teach godly principles with an eternal perspective that go against our culture. It would be really easy for any of us to be angry at God when we go through trials and testings. It would be really easy to grow bitter. Often we do grow bitter and angry.

Our culture reminds us constantly that we deserve happiness. Our culture claims that we all are winners—no one loses. Our culture teaches us to be entitled. But in reality, we don't deserve anything. It goes against our culture to have joy in the midst of sorrow and pain. It goes against our culture to be grateful. It goes against our culture to trust God no matter what. And it goes against our culture to believe that God can be good all the time. But the greatest freedom is when we can get to that place where we can say in confidence, "God is sovereign. God is good. God is good ALL the time."

We will all face challenges in our lives. Whether they are health issues, crumbling marriages, or financial struggles, we will all face trials of some sort. Our culture says that we deserve to be happy and that we should feed our own happiness and well-being. But often it is in those trials and testings, in our desert experiences, that God is doing something so much bigger. God is refining us. God is teaching us to trust Him.

Today, kids are going off to college unable to function in

But the greatest freedom is when we can get to that place where we can say in confidence, "God is sovereign. God is good. God is good ALL the time."

society because we as parents have put so much pressure on them that by the time they arrive to college, they are depressed, dependent, and feel like failures. We cater to them, do everything for them, and put them on a platform filled with pressure to perform to the point that they are paralyzed by the fear of failure. As moms, we should allow our children to fail. We should let them fail while they are still at home. It is okay for a child to experience both success and failure. In fact, it is healthy and good for them to experience both. It is an important life lesson. We all experience defeat and hard times. Being unfamiliar with experiencing loss or pain can be paralyzing for a child. It is our job as moms to coach them while loving and supporting them through these challenges. An excellent life lesson for any child is that life doesn't always turn out like we want it to or have planned. Defeat, failure, and pain are a part of real life, and helping a child navigate through this kind of loss is a part of parenting that our society tries to avoid.

We do our children a disservice when we teach them that we are all winners and never allow them to experience defeat. Giving everyone on the team a trophy just for showing up is not teaching our children about real life. There is this mentality, whether in sports or even academics, that recognizing success for just one person and not including everyone is taboo. I couldn't disagree more. If we make everyone a winner, then there is no drive to succeed, and we stop working hard. We are all made and created differently and have been given different gifts. And it's

> Parenting is hard work—simply because it is heart work.

also okay that we recognize that we aren't good at everything. We have strengths and weaknesses. This is a very important lesson that is being removed from our children's childhood experiences today. Real life has pain. Real life has struggles. Real life has loss. Real life has consequences. Reaching my child's heart and helping her learn how to navigate both success and failure is a vital part of understanding that God is sovereign and good all the time. We must teach our children to trust God even in the hard times—in the desert experiences of life.

Parenting is hard work—simply because it is *heart* work. When we are invested in reaching a person's heart, it is hard work. Creating a firm and solid foundation that can handle the storms and trials of life takes time. We, as moms, must first be working on creating a strong and firm foundation in our own personal lives to be able to teach those principles to our children. When we begin parenting with an eternal perspective, not only will we go against culture, but we will also help our children own their faith—knowing and understanding what they believe and why they believe it, even in the midst of life's storms. We are helping them build a strong foundation so they can stand firm when storms come. Intentional parenting takes time and patience to look for teachable moments in both the good times and bad. Our desert experiences can be some of the best moments to teach our children to trust God. But we must purposefully see Him in the midst of the pain with an unwavering faith that He is good all the time.

Part III:

Impact and Influence for the Next Generation: Raising World Changers

Motherhood can often feel very overwhelming, like a daunting task that we will never measure up to. Feelings of failure and a lack of success in our daily tasks leave us with a perceived sense of hopelessness. Whether it is in comparing ourselves to others or in seeing our own children struggle, we can easily think that nothing we do matters. We can become defeated all too quickly. But God doesn't want us to feel defeated. We don't have to just survive the parenting years; we were made to thrive. We have already been equipped and given the grace needed to be successful. Although it requires a lot of hard work, motherhood can be a place to flourish in our relationship with Jesus.

> We don't have to just survive the parenting years; we were made to thrive.

Having a blueprint for where we want to end up at the end of our eighteen-year journey with each child will assist us in staying on course with a clear mission and focus. Having a game plan is one of the basic principles of parenting. Casting vision and considering where we are wanting to go takes time, but it is imperative for successful parenting. Proverbs 29:18a (KJV) says, "Where there is no vision, the people perish."

In order for success, we must be confident of our goals as parents. We will face trials and difficult times, and without a clear game plan and vision for our future, we may become despondent and hopeless. Parenting will always have its challenges, but being prepared with a clear vision and understanding our mission and purpose will give us the courage needed to continue pressing forward. Let's purposefully think ahead in creating a strategy for success. We have an opportunity to invest in our child's life for eighteen very short years while they are living under our roof, and we must be intentional in creating a game plan for what those eighteen years look like if we expect to achieve our goals. The opportunity for success becomes greater when we take the time to create a plan.

We have been created for such a time as this. The exact time, place, and location in which we currently live is not a surprise to God. We have been born in the exact time and century He ordained. We live in the nation and culture that God has chosen for us. You are the mother to the exact children God has chosen for you to have. You are chosen for such a time as this. You are the perfect mother for your children. God makes no mistakes.

We are called and chosen and fully equipped for our role in motherhood. We have been tasked with this high calling, but this calling is also a gift. Often we neglect or dismiss gifts. Let's pause and appreciate the gifts we are given.

We have an opportunity to literally impact this generation and leave our handprint on future generations. As mothers, we can change the trajectory of the future as we become intentional in reaching our children's hearts for Jesus.

> We have an opportunity to literally impact this generation and leave our handprint on future generations.

We must understand that we are in a spiritual battle. Marriages are under attack. Our families are under attack. Our children are being attacked. We must understand that as mothers we are engaged in a war. We are facing spiritual warfare and we are daily on the battlefront in our role as mothers. We must stand firm and fight this battle, understanding fully who we are in Christ. Our children are not the enemy. Parenting is spiritual warfare. The enemy, Satan, wants our children. Our culture wants our children. We must fight to protect them and raise up a godly generation. As we go to battle, we must be fully prepared, putting on the full armor of God to be ready to fight.

The battle is fought on our knees in prayer. There is power in the name of Jesus. But we must believe that we have access to that power as heirs of God. As we understand the authority and power we have as children of the King of Kings, we will begin to pray with authority. As mothers, we have the opportunity to raise up a generation who knows who they are in Christ and who are fully suited for battle. We must prepare our children for battle. In Jesus' name, we fight this war to protect our marriages, our children, and our families.

The earlier we can help our children understand that they are sinners in need of a Savior, the better job we can do in reaching their hearts and preparing them for this spiritual battle. Once we get to the point that our children can take ownership for their actions and attitude and come into a personal relationship with Jesus, then they can join us as we begin to fight this battle together. Remember, parenting is a spiritual battle. Our children are not the enemy.

> Parenting is a spiritual battle. Our children are not the enemy.

When our children have a personal relationship with Jesus, then the Holy Spirit is at work in and through them. We have the Holy Spirit on our side convicting them; you aren't doing all the work! When we reach a child's heart early, and we can lay a really strong foundation, parenting becomes easier as they move into teenage years. But when we don't take the time to lay a strong foundation in those early years, then we have to start playing catch up and do damage control in addition to building the foundation. Of course, our children will still have struggles and battles, even with a personal relationship with Jesus. But the challenges become easier when we can partner together as parent and child with the power of the Holy Spirit in this spiritual battle.

Moms, you are created for such a time as this. You are raising up world changers! Reaching your children's heart for Jesus, equipping them, and praying for them is essential. We live in a world full of fear and danger. Parenting is spiritual warfare, and we're in a battle. Fear can be all consuming if at any point we take our eyes off Jesus. Our identity and foundation must be secure in knowing who we are in Christ. Fear is from the enemy, Satan. He wants us to live and operate from a place of fear. If he can keep us bound in the bondage of fear, we will be paralyzed and unable to fight this battle with confidence.

God is sovereign. The battle belongs to the Lord. We know who wins in the end. We know how this story will ultimately conclude. Resting in the sovereignty of God and knowing that He is in control, regardless of what surrounds us, gives us peace in the midst of any storm. The world we live in can leave us feeling discouraged and afraid. There is war and terror. There is evil everywhere we turn. Our world is full of callous and heinous wickedness, and it's easy to feel defeat. But we must remember we are already told in Ephesians 6:12, "For our struggle is not against flesh and blood, but against the rulers, against the authorities, against the powers of this dark world and against the spiritual forces of evil in the heavenly realms."

Moms, we must know who we are fighting. We must have a solid grasp on our identity being founded in Christ. As we claim the authority we are granted in

> Moms, you are created for such a time as this. You are raising up world changers!

the name of Jesus, as royal heirs in the family of God, we face this spiritual warfare with confidence. This doesn't mean that we won't have trials or that bad things won't happen. In fact, quite the opposite is true. We know we will face trials. We know we will face persecution. We are warned of this: "I have told you these things, so that in me you may have peace. In this world you will have trouble.

But take heart! I have overcome the world" (John 16:33). The question isn't about avoiding trouble but whether we know who we are fighting and how to fight. We can rest in the fact that God is in control. God is sovereign, and He sits on the throne.

> We are raising up an army for God and must equip them for spiritual warfare.

It is from this place of understanding that we see our children with potential. It is from our calling and commission to make disciples that we see the army of world changers we are training. We are raising up an army for God and must equip them for spiritual warfare. As mothers, we see our role with a great sense of purpose as we fully embrace the high calling of motherhood. We have been called. We are chosen. There is no accident or mistake. We have the opportunity to raise up leaders who will impact the world for Christ. A mother's influence has the potential for impacting a family, a community, a culture, and a future generation. We can literally touch the world as we make disciples in our own homes. Our impact and reach is endless.

Chapter 8

GAME PLAN FOR MOTHERHOOD

A YEAR BEFORE WE ARE scheduled to depart, the planning begins. Hours are spent in giddy excitement as my three princesses and husband map out what the week will look like. Endless hours are spent online making reservations to ensure that nothing is missed and every minute of every day is maximized to its fullest. My husband is a huge Disney fan. He loves everything and all things Disney. He has trained our girls from birth to appreciate our Disney vacations and the "Imagineering" behind this special company. It's more than the magic or the escape from real life for a week; it's an appreciation for the art and creativity behind this particular company. It's the appreciation for excellence that is expected to be maintained at all times in order to provide the experience that Disney fans have come to appreciate. There are many theme parks in America, but it is the Walt Disney Company that has been able to successfully provide an "experience" with each visit. They are intentional not only in the big picture but also in every single minute detail. It is this full package—the pristine park atmosphere, the expectation that the customer is always right, the requirement that cast members stay in character at all times—that ensures that customers will return by the thousands, year after year.

We are one of those families that recognize and appreciate this kind of excellence and therefore anticipate our Disney vacation experiences. If Disney were just mediocre, we would not return. But because Disney takes such care in the detail of the experience from start to finish, we do return. They think of everything! A few years ago, Disney added the customer service feature of delivering your luggage to your room. They identify your luggage when you drop it off at the airport, pick it up from baggage claim for you, drive it to the Disney resort, and place it neatly in your hotel room. As a mom, this became one of the greatest features in the Disney experience! The company is into details. And with that kind of mindset, always looking to be intentional and purposeful with every single experience, they set themselves apart. They are truly head and shoulders above any other company because of taking this kind of attention to detail.

The planning process, mapping out the week of character meals and fast passes, is almost as much fun as the week of vacation. As we begin to plot and plan each dining experience, choose which fast passes will be selected for each day, and draft a plan of attack to make the most of every day and capitalize on each hour (of course, maximizing those extra magic hours), we get silly with excitement just thinking about the fun we will have. If a park is open until 3:00 AM, you can be sure that our family of five is in the park until 3:00 AM—not only to make the most of our day and time at Walt Disney World but also because it's part of the fun!

Needless to say, the full Disney experience requires a calculated and thought-out plan of attack. While stressful for some, it's not stressful for us. It's an important and enjoyable part of the process of experiencing a week of vacation at the Happiest Place on Earth. Without this calculated time of mapping out and planning our days, we would miss out on so much. While we do keep each day flexible and always allow time for spontaneity, having a plan allows us to make the most of our trip!

Like planning that perfect Disney vacation, we may have a lot of fun along the way in the world of parenthood but, without taking the time to plan, we may miss a lot that there is to see or do. We need to know where we are going and how we plan to get there. We have the opportunity to map out what we want parenting to look like. We have to strategize and create a game plan to ensure that we are intentional in our parenting goals, not missing any milestones along the way.

We may not win every battle. We will have some defeats and failures, but we can never take our eyes off the prize—the end goal at the conclusion of the eighteen years with our children under our roof. Our desire is to successfully launch capable and independent young adults with a solid biblical worldview to pursue the plans and places God is calling them.

We are working ourselves out of a job as mothers, so how do we reach that kind of success? At what point is our work done? If our goal is to launch successful young adults into the world with a strong biblical worldview and a firm understanding of what they believe and why they believe it, how will we know we have reached success?

Over the course of the last few years of public speaking, one of my favorite analogies to share is that of a sports team preparing for the new season. Even moms can appreciate a good game of football, whether college or professional. Personally, I think college football is a lot more exciting to watch, but we are going to use the NFL since that is their profession and career. When the NFL season begins, the coaching staff's entire purpose and planning for the team is all about winning and making it to the Super Bowl. There is absolutely nothing in their strategy that takes the team on an alternate course. Everything that a coach demands of his players is with one goal and one purpose in mind—winning the Super Bowl. Every team has the same purpose and same goal, but only two teams will earn a coveted spot to compete.

There are different strategies, different training regiments, and different coaching approaches, but the goal is the same. Every team wants to take home the coveted Super Bowl trophy, and the individual players want those Super Bowl rings. With every game, winning or losing, the team keeps the goal of making it to the playoffs in the forefront of their minds. Adjustments are made each week. In the locker room, a coach will have the team watch videos of plays from the week before, not only analyzing their own successes and shortcomings but also watching their opponents' games, studying them just as intently, preparing to meet their opposition the coming week.

A good NFL team will never lose sight of their goal and their mission. Even in the midst of defeat or loss, a dedicated team will study harder and make preparations to go out and fight with more passion and vigor the next week. The team knows what their goal is, and they never ever take their eyes off the prize. Everything they do on the field and off the field is in preparation for winning. Each player spends time training to be in the very best condition to meet the opponent each week. Every player and coaching staff heads to the field with a sense of purpose. They have a goal, and that goal is to win.

Motherhood is much like playing for the NFL. There is risk involved. There can be pain. There is serious dedication. We can get hurt. But the reward can be great. Like football, there is an opponent and a battle to be fought. We must train diligently, preparing for each and every day, working hard to fight for our mission in parenting. We must stay focused and keep our eyes on the prize. Even in the off-season, players are still staying fit, eating right, and training for the next season. Parents don't get an off-season, but like those football players, we too must stay focused day after day, month after month, year after year.

As your child gets older and grows, you make yearly adjustments. You fine-tune your strategy and game plan. Discipline may become less frequent as your child gets older, but conversations about life will increase. The transition of demanding a child to obey will change to a more thoughtful approach in the teen years as we allow our children to question why we have rules in place and then discuss the reasons with them. Moreover, as our children get older, we have the opportunity to help them navigate their own worldview and understand the world around them. We discuss sin and the consequences of sin and the principle of reaping what we sow.

As parents, we are blessed to help steer our children's maturity and growth, transitioning them successfully from a child into an adult. But just like the NFL or a trip to Disney World, this requires a game plan and quite a bit of hard work. We need to be strategic and thoughtful. We need to know what we want our child to look like at eighteen, and then we need to back up and create a plan for how we intend to get there. We must keep our eyes on the goal that we hope to achieve and continue to make adjustments along the way.

My favorite class at Baylor University was an entrepreneurship class that I took one summer. I loved the professor, and although it was not a part of my major, it resonated with me. It was one of those classes that just seemed practical and offered common sense lessons for all areas of life. At the time, I had no interest or desire to go into any kind of business, much less start a company. I am, however, a visionary. I love breaking the mold. An entrepreneur has to be able to have a vision and have a willingness to take the risk to create something from nothing. An entrepreneur must be willing to fail but will never let a loss determine the outcome. She will never ever doubt that success is possible. A good entrepreneur will stay focused and determined on what is at stake, with a willingness to be committed to the venture no matter what. A true entrepreneur will never accept defeat but will always find a way to succeed. She is creative and will think outside the box to meet goals and find success.

Creativity is important in entrepreneurship. Creativity in parenting is important as well. Being able to think differently, seeing life from distinct perspectives, is a gift from God. Because we are all unique individuals, our parenting strategies and decisions will also be unique for our own families. There is not a cookie-cutter parenting approach in life. Our own personalities, combined with the individuality of each child within our family, will force us to parent our children differently. We have the same end result in mind—reaching each child's heart for Jesus—but how we get there can look very different for each one.

Just as each coach and coaching staff for a football team will bring in new and different approaches that are reflective of their personalities, we too will be creative in how our parenting looks. We need to give a lot of grace in how others parent their children. Our families aren't going to all look the same. While we should be working toward the same goals, how we reach them may take a different course because our children are all different and because we, as parents, are all different.

One approach that I've used often when invited to a speaking engagement is the idea of an enterprise. I love public speaking and the opportunity it gives me to take moms on the journey of envisioning and building something special in their homes. I like to get moms to be forward thinking by creating a vision for the lives of their children. When we think of building something, such as an enterprise, we first step back and decide what it is we're trying to create. Entrepreneurs love this because the idea of creating something out of nothing is exhilarating. In the corporate world, there would be mission statements and vision statements, quarterly meetings, taking inventory, and analyzing successes and areas needing improvement. There would be goals and benchmarks driving success.

When the girls were very young, my husband and I would periodically get a babysitter and go to a local coffee shop to discuss each one of our individual princesses. We would take inventory of areas that Reagan, Jordan, and Riley were successful in, such as first-time obedience or sharing. We would also discuss areas in which they needed to make improvements, such as their attitude or kindness toward one another. Setting aside this time for intentional conversation gave us very tangible and real opportunities to focus our discipline and discipleship.

This focused time also gave us an opportunity, as a couple, to get on the same page in our approach to parenting. It helped me to step back from the day-to-day of seeing my children up close to an aerial view of seeing that we were actually making progress. Sometimes, when we are in the middle of parenting, we get so lost in the minutia that we lose sight of the big picture. Taking a few hours over coffee with my husband allowed me to see life from a different vantage point. Not only could we address the areas where we could continue to work, but we could also see that our girls were making progress and becoming successful in many ways. This kind of analysis is the same thing that an enterprise or company would do in their quarterly meetings. It just gives us that big picture approach in bite sized pieces. We are willing to take the time to see the good and the bad. It gives us hope and practical and tangible ways to grow. It allows us to become more focused in our discipline and discipleship.

More often than not, a father is not home and around for much of the discipline or discipleship of our children. They are busy at work, coming in after bedtime or with just enough time to join the bedtime ritual. And some fathers miss much of the weekday activities due to work-related travel, only being home on the weekends. I am so incredibly grateful for my husband's hard work to provide for our family. I am grateful for his job. At the same time, I want him to enjoy our girls' childhoods and be invested in their upbringing. He has so much to offer in ways that I can't. Making him a part of this team approach to parenting is really important to me. Figuring out how to keep our husbands a part of the day-to-day of our children's lives can be challenging, but it is so healthy and good when our husbands can be fully present and engaged as fathers.

Side note for our single moms: I know it's not easy. For whatever reason you are single, whether by death or divorce or simply by choice, you are not overlooked! You have it that much harder, doing life and carrying the load as a single mother, providing not only financially but also emotionally, being fully present as a mother. My hat's off to you! You are doing a great job!

> A lack of communication in parenting can become a wedge in the marriage.

I hear a lot of moms complain that their husbands aren't on the same page as they are when it comes to discipline or reinforcing what they have been working on all day. The mother becomes the "bad guy" at the end of the day when dad comes home from work ready to be the superhero who gets the kids to laugh endlessly with his rambunctious antics. Communication is vital for successful parenting. But part of the challenge is making time for communication to ensure we are on the same page and working toward the same goals for success. Often, parenting can become divisive in a marriage relationship, primarily because we are not being intentional to be on the same page in our parenting goals. Instead of serving together in a team approach, a lack of communication in parenting can become a wedge in the marriage.

Frequently, our husbands will be away at work all day and come home only to step on a landmine when he walks in the door. One of the things that I encourage mothers to do is to have a quick five-minute phone call with her husband when he is on the way home from work, giving him the lay of the land. Give him a head's up and tell him which child needs help with homework, who needs a bath, who is staying late after school for sport's practice, and possibly who needs a talk about attitude and behavior. This short phone call will allow you and your husband to connect, get on the same page, and avoid any potential explosions when he walks in the door. If he can come home knowing the lay of the land, he can be ready to assist and ready to help instead of being bombarded with unexpected questions and demands and not responding the way you hoped. This short phone call will also ensure and reinforce to a child that you are united in your parenting and that playing one parent against the other will never be tolerated or allowed. Having a proactive strategy to parenting, rather than a reactive response, will help us move to a more intentional approach in our parenting.

> Having a proactive strategy to parenting, rather than a reactive response, will help us move to a more intentional approach in our parenting.

Marriage is hard. Parenting is hard. Marriage is two sinners living under the same roof. It's no wonder marriage is so hard. Then we bring more "little sinners"—our children—into the family. Now we have a house full of sinners trying not to kill one another.

In case you didn't know, your kids are actually born sinners. They do not *become* sinners; they are sinners from birth. They are selfish little beings that want to claim your undivided attention and be the center of the universe. So it makes sense that our culture is made up of selfish families. We have households full of sinners, all selfish, all imperfect, living under the same roof.

Many of us are still in the early years of marriage, our honeymoon phase, when we embark on the journey of parenting. Even for those who wait a while to have kids, all couples are still learning to navigate basic principles like sharing, compromising, and getting along with one another when we bring a child into our world. Now we compound our own selfishness with a lack of sleep and a lack of knowledge, and what we have is a bunch of barely-functioning adults in charge of raising little people to become successful adults.

Most people I talk to enter into parenting without a game plan. We grow up with the expectation that we will get a good job, marry, and have children. We put a lot of prep time and hard work into our academics and earning a good job, but we often enter into marriage and parenthood without a game plan for success. We go into these relationships—the most important relationships—having no idea what to do. Most of the time, we rely on what was modeled for us. We just try to figure it out as we go, entering into these relationships unprepared and without vision.

How do we develop a game plan for parenting, working toward the goal of unity in our parenting approach? Companies, life coaches, marketing strategists, and authors will do what is called storyboarding. This is a process of putting up pictures or words or ideas on a big board to create a story. It allows us to visualize the strategy of getting from point A to point B. It gives us something tangible to see and move toward.

In the case of parenting, imagine with me that you set up four different poster boards. On each board, we would include physical growth, emotional growth, intellectual growth, and spiritual growth. We would include ways we want to see our child grow and succeed as a whole person. We would put up pictures or words or ideas for what our child's success would look like at marked stages. We would identify goals to cover the child as a whole person. We would look at the big picture and know what we want our child to do and be by age eighteen. Then we would begin to back things up and create smaller, age-appropriate goals on each storyboard, ultimately moving toward a larger list of goals for success by the time the child is ready to launch.

The first poster board will represent the first five years of life—the foundational years. On this board, I would put up pictures of a baby's physical and cognitive growth and development, such as a child toilet training, learning to read, and memorizing Bible verses. We could also include pictures or words for a child exhibiting first-time obedience, respect, care and concern for others, and coming when called. We might put up a picture of a child setting the table or putting away laundry. We are simply displaying on this board some goals that we want to see our infant reach by five years of age. Early on, we set goals and create a game plan.

Moreover, if my child is five years old and not ready to move on to the second storyboard, I can still look at the upcoming storyboard to assess our progress. I can see if we are on task and what work still needs to be done. I can also assess what my child is doing well and identify the areas we need to spend more time on before we can move on to storyboard number two. As I look at storyboard number two, I become keenly aware of the things that I want to begin teaching my child. Storyboarding is giving me vision and practical goals for success in parenting my child as a whole person. I am calculated to make sure that I'm reaching the heart while also training my child to be a successful adult by the time we reach storyboard number four. My goal is to see each one of my children launch well.

We would label the second board the elementary years, for the ages 6-11 range. This board would include our children's primary years of schooling. Here, goals may include participating in extracurricular activities like a sports team, learning a musical instrument, reading the Bible on their own, memorizing Scripture, reading books on grade level at home in addition to what is being assigned at school, participating in Sunday school and church, consistency in first-time obedience, demonstrating a helpful attitude around the house, keeping their rooms cleaned, making their own bed, cleaning the bathrooms, mopping the kitchen floor, practicing early financial responsibility, etc.

Again, you see, we are covering the child as a whole person, envisioning age-appropriate tasks that we want them to be successful at by eleven years old. We're breaking down the parenting process into tangible and attainable goals, but we must continue to model these behaviors for them. If we want them to know how to help around the house, we have to teach them how to clean a bathroom and how to do it well. We are helping them learn to take responsibility and to be a contributing part of the family. I, as the mother, will not be the only person who cleans our house; we will all contribute toward this effort as a family.

Our third storyboard would cover ages 12-15. It may look something like having pictures of a child taking responsibility for yard work, cleaning bathrooms, washing dishes, doing homework, reading, participating in sports, playing a musical instrument or being in choir. It could include being involved in a Bible study or church youth group, going to camp, memorizing Scripture, taking leadership opportunities, having a heart to serve others well, or volunteering community service hours.

These early teen years are so important, and having a game plan for these teen years is critical. It's not just about keeping them busy and occupying their time. It's all about reaching their heart and looking at the trajectory of their life. We are in the home stretch after this, so these years are absolutely essential to a successful launch. It is frequently during these teen years when parents struggle with a child's attitude and behavior the most. For this reason, it is important that we are seriously aware of their attitude at this point. While this is something we want to be mindful of at each stage of development, it is one of the most important aspects of this particular age. Parents wonder why their kids aren't talking with them anymore or don't want to spend time with them. Part of this is reflective of the early foundational years in how we parented, but part of it is also a child's normal and healthy growth toward autonomy and independence. We must intentionally keep the door of communication open and active.

These are the years that we don't want to excuse their behavior, saying, "They are just being teenagers." This is when we must become even more intentional in our time and conversation with our children. If we are having good conversation around the dinner table, then we are talking with our kids about their worldview. We are discussing world affairs and are able to get a glimpse into how they are processing life. These years are paramount! Communication and time are the keys to reaching a teenager. Ensuring their heart is soft and growing in their relationship with the Lord will be a defining outcome in how they begin to create their own worldview. It is at this point that their faith is becoming their own and less dependent on us as parents. We want our teens to begin to be able to defend their faith and to know what they believe and why they believe it. We want them to be able to stand on their own two feet before they leave home.

The fourth and final storyboard would be for ages 16-18 years. This storyboard would include anything and everything that you want your children to have accomplished, learned, or experienced before they leave home. You would include things about who they are as a person and what you are working on teaching them. What is their attitude like? How does their personal relationship with the Lord look? What is it that you want to teach them about life? The pictures could include money and finances, cooking, cleaning, mowing a yard, and being well read. It might also include academics, applying to colleges, making decisions, grocery shopping, getting a job, knowing how to drive, etc. This list is endless. Most importantly, it would include their ability to articulate what they believe and why they believe it. It would include a picture of a young person who is a leader and isn't easily swayed by peers. It should include a firm foundation of their worldview.

Using the idea of storyboarding can give you, as a mother, tangible goals to set that will help you continue parenting with intention. Once you have your storyboard in place, you then can come up with a game plan for success. *Now that I know where I am going, I can determine how I am going to get there.*

At this point, reader, you are probably wondering if my home office is covered with storyboards for each one of my daughters. The answer is no. However, while I have not literally hung up storyboards for each child, I have done this exact exercise mentally. Years ago, when our daughters were very young, I began mentally mapping out these very things. Storyboarding is just one possible tool. If it helps you to have a tangible and visual plan, then it may be helpful for you to create actual storyboards. Or, if it's more practical, you can create a notebook. If you don't need the visual, you should still take the time mentally to take inventory of where you are going and how you plan to get there.

It is important to remember that while there may be several areas in which we desire all our kids to learn and grow, the individual storyboards for each child should look a little different. There are things that each one of our children will be working on individually because they are individuals. Their personalities and interests vary, so we want to make sure we reach each child individually and not assume that one size fits all. For example, if I have one daughter who is shy, teaching her how to be confident and speak up in public will be a goal that I will work on with her, but I may or may not have to spend as much time on this goal with my other children. Every child is a unique individual, and we need to parent them as such.

What is the mission of your home? Where do you see your children five, ten, or fifteen years from now? When we have a clear idea of where we are headed, then we begin to calculate backwards to determine tangible goals for success. Oftentimes, we end up at their high school graduation and think of all the things we could have done better or wish we could do over. When our kids are born, or even when they are starting school, we typically don't take the time to think through just how short the amount of time is that we actually have with them. Then one day, graduation arrives. They feel ready to leave, but we aren't ready for them to leave. Having a game plan and parenting with intention and purpose allows us as parents to be very thoughtful in how we order our days.

We each have our own unique family with its own set of strengths and challenges. But if we are striving to reach our children's heart for Jesus, then the process of what that looks like can be beautiful for each of us. Some of us like to color outside the lines, while others feel strongly to stay inside the lines. While it may look quite messy from our vantage point, God is looking down from above and can see a masterpiece in the making.

As we set out to create a game plan for motherhood, my approach may look very different from your approach. That's all good! No matter the colors you use to paint your picture and regardless if you like abstract art or a more classic painting, my challenge to you is to develop a game plan before you put brush to paper. Think strategy. How do you plan to spend the eighteen years that you are given with your gift? Keep in mind that art can be messy. Before the painting is complete, it may look nothing like the intended result. However, a patient artist sees the end result long before others. The artist can visualize the masterpiece and is very deliberate and thoughtful with each stroke of the brush. Parenting is much like a messy work of art for much of our eighteen years, but in the end a masterpiece has been created.

When we coddle our children to the point of preventing them from growing up independently and appropriately, we no longer do what is best for them. If we want our middle-school aged children to become mature adults, we must begin giving them some responsibility and appropriate freedoms while they are still at home to help them navigate this independence responsibly. We need to have a game plan and know what it is we want from our children by the time they leave home and go off to college. When we have a game plan, we can figure out a strategy to reach those goals. By casting vision, I become less concerned about what everyone else is doing because I am on a mission for where I am going with my family. I understand that I am called to the high calling of motherhood for the children I have—not your children, but my children. I have a purpose and vision for where I am headed in discipleship and discipline. I can cheer for you, but I won't compare my children or circumstance to you. I am too busy creating my own masterpiece.

Chapter 9

ESTHER MOMENT: FOR SUCH A TIME AS THIS

WHAT IF? THOSE TWO WORDS can be crippling. The chance to take a risk often results in a barrage of various "what if?" questions. I can lie in bed at night and think of every single "what if" possible. In fact, I have. Why is it that, in the dark of the night, fear lurks around every corner? Moms, let's be honest. We all lie in bed and think of some of the most extreme "what if" scenarios for our children. While these might be extreme examples, the very real risks associated with parenting create an excess of "what if" scenarios on a daily basis. The very fact that I am a mother means I have risks. I have literally not been able to fall asleep at night because of these two words. Or I have woken up in the middle of the night with the thought of these scenarios and have broken out in a cold sweat. These two words can create fear. But without risk, we can't live life to the fullest. Life is full of risk. Risk is learning to let go. Risk is learning to let your children do things on their own for the first time. Risk is allowing your kids to grow up. Motherhood is full of risk!

I guess you can say that I have always been a risk taker. I was the kid who wanted a broken arm more than anything. I would actually seek out a tree, climb to the top, and jump. I would even try to land on my arm in order to break it! The cast, the attention, the fun—it would be worth the pain, I thought. I guess all that milk I drank as a kid gave me really strong bones, and I never broke my arm. I was a thrill-seeker. Sometimes I would climb to the top of the roof of our single-story house and jump off. You know, just for fun. It was a thrill. It was that feeling of just enough danger without really ever being at a place of getting hurt. It was the daredevil in me that liked living on the edge, breaking the mold, and being me. I was actually very obedient at home and in school and never really got in any trouble; but, inwardly, I always wanted my independence. If everyone in the entire class was going to wear matching t-shirts, I was definitely *not* going to wear that shirt. I hate conformity. I like breaking the mold. I hate being put in a box or being like everyone else. I want to be my own person.

Now, as with all risk, sometimes there are natural consequences. When I was in fifth grade, our school class took a field trip to a local park for the day. We took packed lunches and rode the bus to a city park. Our class spent the day playing on the playground and exploring the nature trails. Well, like any good nature trail, all of the plants, flowers, and trees were clearly marked and labeled—not only with their scientific classification but also with their common name. There could be no questioning what each plant was. And so, a group of us came upon a plant identified as "Poison Ivy." Of course, like the other plants, it was clearly marked and identified. Being one who enjoyed living life on the edge and loving a good opportunity to take a risk, especially with an audience, I spoke up and announced loudly to the group of fifth graders gathered around, "Hey, watch this!" I then proceeded to break off several leaves of the poison ivy branch and rub them all over my entire body.

I had never had poison ivy before, so I was curious. It seemed like a great idea! After going through four or five leaves, I grabbed another big handful and thoroughly rubbed down my entire body— arms, legs, stomach, and face. Once I felt confident that I had fully covered myself, we continued making our way down the nature trail. I played all day with friends, proud to be the one who took the risk and braved the dreaded poison ivy leaves.

Risk. Like I said, some risks have natural consequences, very natural consequences. And what do you know? I actually got poison ivy! I got it so bad that I had to go to the doctor the very next day to get a shot just to help get rid of it. It felt like the worst case of poison ivy on the planet. I got it bad! My fifth-grade teacher was hosting a party at her house the next day, and I was unable to attend. Instead, I was stuck inside, and my only outing for the next several days was to see the doctor to assess the consequences of my risk. Now you may ask if I regret taking that risk. Of course not! It's part of my story!

When I was about thirteen years old, I felt God speak into my heart during a personal time in prayer, telling me that I would have an orphanage one day. From the time I was a small child, I wanted to grow up to be a mom. I absolutely loved kids! I loved being around babies and kids of any age. I loved to babysit, work in the church nursery, and just be with kids any opportunity I was given. So, an orphanage made sense to me because I loved kids so much. Although I participated in several mission trips, I never felt convicted that this orphanage would be outside of the United States. I just believed with all my heart that God had told me that I would have an orphanage one day. Anyone who knew me knew this was the plan. I was very outspoken about it and confident God would make this happen. I was bold in my belief, actually choosing my major in college with this plan in mind. I had faith.

Once I felt God had spoken this promise in my heart, it was my mission. It was the frame of reference for every decision I made. I didn't know when, where, or how. But I believed. Shortly after I graduated from college, I gathered a group of twelve ladies, all moms that I respected, and asked them to commit to pray for me for an entire year for this orphanage God had planted in my heart. I figured if Jesus had twelve disciples, I would have my twelve prayer disciples.

To be honest, I had no idea what this plan would really look like. If people thought I was crazy, they didn't let on. They appeared to believe in me and were waiting for this big day to happen. If God spoke, I was going to be willing and ready. Faith and risk. I was ready to step out in faith and take a risk.

I had been out of college for a couple of years, still living and working in Texas. It was during this time that my brother introduced me to one of his best friends who was wrapping up his senior year at Baylor University—Todd. One warm Texas evening in April, I met a group of friends who had gathered in an apartment on campus. I was pleased to see Todd there, as well, and enough flirting occurred between us that we left everyone else and headed down the street to Common Grounds, a coffee shop on the edge of campus. This was our first date. Early in our dating when we began talking about getting married, I told Todd that I felt God was going to give me an orphanage one day. I also told him I had no idea what this meant, what it would look like, or how or when it would happen. But he needed to understand that the only way we could get married was if he were agreeable to the idea. In my mind, I couldn't marry him unless he could believe this promise from God to me. By complete faith, he agreed and was all in.

Within a few short months, Todd and I were engaged. We were married within a year. By the time we started having children, the idea of an orphanage had completely died. Still, I never questioned that God had spoken to me as a young girl. At this time, however, there was just nothing in me looking for or desiring an orphanage. I always believed; I just no longer had any desire. My girls were all that mattered. But I still believed that God had given me a promise. While the promise remained real in my heart, the desire and dream for an orphanage had completely died.

One of my favorite stories in the Bible is about an orphan. Esther was a young Jewish girl who had been orphaned and was cared for by her cousin, Mordecai. Her people, the Jews, needed deliverance. She ends up in a position of influence before the king. Her cousin says to her, "Do not think that because you are in the king's house you alone of all the Jews will escape. For if you remain silent at this time, relief and deliverance for the Jews will arise from another place, but you and your father's family will perish. And who knows but that you have come to your royal position for such a time as this?" (Esther 4:13b–14). I absolutely love this story because it was an orphan, completely parentless, who had been given an opportunity to serve God in such a big way.

Mordecai essentially told Esther that God would keep His promise to deliver His people, with or without her, but her position of influence gave her the opportunity to be used by God to impact an entire group of people—God's chosen people, the Jews. It wasn't just about Esther, but rather, Esther was in a place of influence for a larger purpose. Our lives aren't about us; they are about God and His purposes. Esther had been chosen and placed in a position of influence by God. He was opening doors for her to impact a generation and the future. God always keeps His promises!

As Mordecai suggests, "perhaps" Esther was created "for such a time as this." But there is no "perhaps" in God's plans. No, God was and is sovereign. Esther's place as an orphan was deliberately used for His glory by putting her in Mordecai's care. In God's sovereignty, Esther was then placed in a position to go before the king and have influence. Because she was available "for such a time as this," her faithfulness left a legacy that has impacted all of history. She, a seemingly insignificant orphan, changed the trajectory of the Jewish people and became part of the lineage of Jesus. What a powerful story! God used this orphan to fulfill His promise to the Jews—His chosen people. Esther was chosen by God for such a time as this!

Likewise, you are a mom chosen for such a time as this. God has placed you in this exact place and time and culture in history with your specific children for a purpose. There are no accidents with God. What will you do with this knowledge? Will you be obedient to God's plan for you and your children? Are you faithfully influencing your children with an eternal perspective? Perhaps your story and your legacy as a mother will impact a culture and a generation to come? Are you embracing your "for such a time as this" moment?

It's not an accident that we were born in the time that we live in today. You aren't an accident. Your children aren't an accident. We do not live in this particular generation or culture by accident. If God can use an orphan to impact the entire Jewish people, then God can use a mom to influence and impact her children who can also change the trajectory of a generation. As moms we must be willing, just as Esther was willing, to obey God and let Him use us in the position He places us. Can you imagine the impact we as moms can have on an entire generation and culture if we are available? We must never underestimate our power of influence for such a time as this. We are a part of a story—God's story—and our position of influence can absolutely change a family, a nation, a culture, or an entire generation.

> Are you embracing your "for such a time as this" moment?

Although I always wanted to be a mom my whole life, a part of me is still fearful to embrace motherhood. I get worried about what my girls' own experiences of motherhood will be like because of the uncertainties and violence we face in the world today. Persecution abounds. Violence runs rampant. Terror and fear are lurking around every corner. But then I am reminded of God's promises and His plan "for such a time as this." Moms have faced heartache and sadness since the beginning of time. The condition of our world, the evil and violence, is not new. Mothers have given birth and raised families in conditions far worse. God still sits on the throne!

Eve, the first mother, faced the heartache of losing a son at the hands of another son. The very first children, brothers, fought to the death. What if? What if Eve had stopped having babies? What if Eve had been too heartbroken to conceive again? What if she didn't trust in God's redemption and His sovereignty? It was through Seth, Eve's third son, that the Bible records the line of Noah. And it was through him and his family that humanity was saved at the time of the flood. Moreover, it was through the line of Seth that God sent Jesus, the ultimate sacrifice and redemption for mankind. And what if Moses' mother, Jochebed, had been too afraid to hide her newborn son when Pharaoh ordered all young male babies to be killed? What if Jochebed had not taken a chance, a huge risk, to put her newborn son into a basket to float down the river into the hands of Pharaoh's daughter? What if this young mother was not willing to let another young woman raise her son? Without these risks, Moses would not have been put into a position to lead the Israelites out of Egypt. Our stories are big. Our stories are complicated. Motherhood involves risk. Motherhood involves trusting God even when we can't see the end result.

Shortly after our third daughter, Riley, was born, our church was beginning a new marriage initiative. The program matched couples who had been married for a minimum of five years with other couples who were either struggling in their marriages or who were just looking to enhance and improve their marriages. Since Todd and I were passionate about marriage and the family, we quickly volunteered to serve. This led to a seven-year journey, including leading the entire program for a few years and teaching marriage classes. We loved the opportunity to invest in other couples, encouraging them that their struggles, while certainly challenging, were not the end. Marriage could not only survive, it could thrive! Marriages that seemed destroyed could be restored by God's grace. With God, anything is possible, including the complete restoration of broken relationships.

> Happiness is based on circumstances, but joy is a condition of the heart.

Looking back, I can clearly see how we were called for such a time as this. For three of the seven years that we participated in this ministry, we were engaged in our own family struggles—our desert experience. While we were not experiencing marital challenges, we were going through a crisis as a family. Ironically, the more vulnerable I became about our struggles and the journey in the desert, the more women flocked to me for advice and wisdom. Moms could not understand how in the world I maintained joy in the midst of such challenges. Happiness is based on circumstances, but joy is a condition of the heart—an unmovable contentment despite circumstances. It is a reflection of gratitude. I began noticing more and more opportunities for ministry coming my way, simply by being real and vulnerable about our own struggles. No one goes through life exempt from struggles, so when we can talk about them, it allows us to become relatable and real to others.

It was during our desert experience in 2011 that I felt God calling me to begin a ministry dedicated to these mothers who were coming to me for advice for their marriages, parenting, and individual struggles. If so many women were coming to me for help, how could I help them? I had no idea what in the world it would look like over time, but I knew I wanted it to be a ministry that was dedicated to covering the mom as a whole person.

Our struggles often affect multiple areas of our life; so, we have to find a way to be healthy in all areas of our life. Moms have such a place of influence, and yet they multi-task all day every day, so I needed to find a way to minister to the mom in every facet of her life. If I could encourage moms in their marriages and parenting, challenging them to set the bar high and at the same time inspiring them to be thoughtful in their finances, health, and nutrition, moms would be ministered to as a whole person reflecting their 24/7 multi-tasking. I had to find a way not to neglect what we may consider as mundane in our role as mothers. I had to reveal value that, even in the mundane of our every day, there is opportunity to show Jesus to a broken and lost world. The greatest place of influence is a mother in the home. If we can reach the mom, we can reach the family. If we can reach the family, we can change the world.

> The greatest place of influence is a mother in the home. If we can reach the mom, we can reach the family. If we can reach the family, we can change the world.

Due to our own financial circumstances during our desert experience, not only was it a huge step of faith to begin a ministry but also a huge risk. Risk! If this risk failed, it would have very natural consequences. We were already not in a good position financially, so a risk that failed would be devastating. Without an extra dime to our name, I signed a contract to host our very first conference on nothing but faith. I had no idea if moms would come. I didn't have the money to pay for it. I had nothing but a prompting from God and faith. I felt strongly God was telling me that now was the time to step out in faith. Risk!

We hosted our very first Passion4Moms Conference in the fall of 2011. About eighty-five moms joined us for a two-day event in a small hotel conference room in Northern Virginia. The fact that we had eighty-five moms in attendance was a miracle! Signing a contract and hosting a conference was a huge risk. The design of the conference was to bring in speakers who would address topics such as marriage, parenting, spiritual growth, health, nutrition, and finances, always with Jesus in the center of everything we do. Most conferences are one-faceted, but I believed that we needed to be different and speak into the multi-faceted lives of moms. I wanted to see moms given tools for success in all areas of their lives.

Our first year was a huge success! There was definitely an audience not only for this ministry but also for this kind of support and encouragement. A one-of-a-kind, unique ministry was being birthed. The approach to covering the mom as a whole person and this kind of conference was unlike anything we had ever seen anywhere in the world. Embracing the mom as a whole person was a brand new concept, but mothers were hungry for this kind of support to learn and grow. We were definitely on to something.

It was a Friday afternoon in the fall of 2013, and we were getting ready to host our second Passion4Moms Conference. As such, I was spending the afternoon in prayer to prepare for the upcoming event. The entire process of everything related to Passion4Moms was an expression of faith. At the time, we were beginning the process to become an official 501(c)3 non-profit, which was a huge endeavor and miracle in and of itself. In addition, my family was still in the midst of our three-year desert experience and faith journey of trusting God for finances. It was during this time of so many unknowns that I was praying that Friday afternoon, and God spoke to me.

It was exactly like when, as a young teenager, God had told me that I would have an orphanage. It wasn't an audible voice, but I know that

I know that I know that it was God speaking clearly in my heart. I had been praying and waiting in silence when I heard God say to my spirit, "This is the orphanage." I can't explain it. And quite frankly it startled me almost to the point of disbelief. How could this be? I wasn't looking for this. My mind was nowhere near the idea of an orphanage. The idea of an orphanage had died. I wasn't working with kids. I wasn't in a third world country. I wasn't a mom to a hundred orphans. What did this mean? How could this ministry of conferences for moms be "the orphanage"?

Well, to be honest, like Gideon in the Bible who put out a fleece and asked God to prove Himself, I also asked God to give me some kind of confirmation this ministry was the orphanage. I felt like our family was already in too vulnerable of a place to be able to accept such a risk. Risk! We were at a huge place of unknowns, and anything that could add extra risk seemed almost dangerous for our family.

I called Todd to tell him about my time in prayer and conversation with God. Without hesitation, Todd said that if God spoke, I needed to obey and walk in faith. He was fully on board and supportive, knowing what was at stake. The next morning at 7:00 AM, my girlfriend Beth texted me from Michigan and asked if this whole new Passion4Moms thing had something to do with the orphanage I had always talked about! I couldn't believe it. That text turned into an hour-long phone conversation. What was God calling me to? What did this mean? Was this my purpose "for such a time as this"?

Many times when God calls us to do something, it ends up being nothing like what we were expecting or envisioning. Quite frankly, while I never doubted God spoke and said, "This is the orphanage," I have struggled with the idea that planning conferences had anything to do with an orphanage. I just didn't get it. Over the course of the next few months, I kept asking God to show me if this was really Him speaking in my heart because I needed Him to make sense of this for me. Over much time and prayer, I have come to believe that the orphaned state of motherhood in our culture is why we host our annual conferences.

The orphanage was a spiritual reference to the abandoned state of the family and motherhood. The promise of an orphanage had nothing to do with caring for abandoned babies in a house, but everything to do with the spiritual state of motherhood and exhorting a generation of spiritual orphans. Marriages are falling apart. Mothers are no longer valued. We claim we are "just moms" rather than embracing the opportunity to affect and influence the culture. Motherhood has been abandoned, disdained, and orphaned by society and our culture. There is an urgency to call mothers to wake up to a biblical standard for motherhood.

> There is an urgency to call mothers to wake up to a biblical standard for motherhood.

We don't really believe that we are raising world changers. We aren't equipping our children to stand firm for Christ in the face of cultural pressures. In fact, often we are raising spiritual orphans who don't have a personal relationship with Jesus at all. I believe that it is this spiritual responsibility of motherhood that has been orphaned and abandoned by our society. The family has been neglected and is no longer valued. Motherhood is no longer esteemed. We are living in a lost world, with entire families being orphaned from the spiritual family of God.

In the spring of 2016, we hosted our largest Passion4Moms Conference to date, with some 800 moms in attendance. My Esther moment "for such a time as this" was stepping out in faith as a mother, willing to take a risk by beginning a non-profit ministry for moms. I believe with all my heart that this is a fulfillment to the promise God gave me some thirty years ago. Fear could have easily stopped it. Our family was not and has not been in a financial position to carry it. Every step of the ministry has been full of risk and a true step of faith.

So this promise of an orphanage was not answered literally in the construction of a physical refuge for children like I would have thought or imagined. And I believe that it was right for the vision of the orphanage to die for a period of time. In John 12:24 Jesus says, "Very truly I tell you, unless a kernel of wheat falls to the ground and dies, it remains only a single seed. But if it dies, it produces many seeds." Just as is promised, letting that seed die produced more than I could have ever dreamed or imagined. From the time of the original promise, at thirteen, there was an entire pruning and prepping process that God had to do in me before I could see the promise fulfilled. The promise had died, but at no point in time did I ever doubt God had spoken.

More often than not, patience is required as we wait while God is preparing and putting all the pieces into place for us to see a promise come to fruition and be resurrected. Full surrender, a dying to self, is often a part of this time of refining with a willingness to walk in obedience by faith even if it means taking a risk. I firmly believe that our three-year desert experience was God refining us as a family, getting us ready for "Go Time!" Those three years prepared us in ways that only God could do. He was getting us to a place of utter surrender, a place of trust totally and completely in Him, so that we could step out in faith when the time was right and say "Yes" to the risk that

He presented. We had learned to trust God on nothing but faith, and that is all we had when we began this ministry. We had no financial resources; we had nothing but faith in a very big God.

When I signed that first contract in 2011, I had no idea that this ministry was the fulfillment of the promise that God made to me thirty years before. It wasn't until two years later, walking in faith and obedience, that God revealed this was, indeed, the orphanage—the promise. I had to step out in faith and obedience first. Through this entire process, God has done the miraculous. He has allowed this ministry to grow and produce many seeds. God is already doing more than I could ever ask or think or imagine. I know that Passion4Moms is His ministry and the fulfillment of a promise He planted in my young teenage heart.

Esther, an orphan, took a risk. God positioned her to fulfill His promise and plan for His chosen people. We are all capable of being used by God when we are willing to step out in faith and obedience and take a risk. When God calls us to do something for Him, He equips us. We don't have all the answers in advance. It's a risk and an act of faith. But when we are willing to be used by Him, God can do the impossible to accomplish His plans and purposes. For me, I believe that I am created "for such a time as this," to be a part of a movement that can absolutely change the trajectory of the next generation by reaching the family through mothers. I am not unique or special. I'm ordinary, just like every other woman. But I am willing. I believe each and every one of us moms has the potential to impact the world around us if we are willing to take risks when God calls us to do so. When we are willing to walk in faith, God can and will move the mountains and part the seas on our behalf.

> You are a mother for such a time as this!

So often we read the Bible and assume that the miracles that God performed are no longer possible. We look at the men and women in the Bible as heroes but don't take into account that we are also children of God. God is the same yesterday, today, and forever. He can split the seas and move mountains on our behalf, too. Just as God used heroes in the Bible, He can use us today in our own culture and generation. I am His child too, just like my brothers and sisters that have gone before me, and my Father has and will continue to perform miracles for His children. I believe whole heartedly that if God is going to do the impossible through us, then we will see Him do miracles to accomplish His purposes. God is the God of the impossible.

What is it that God has called you to do? What promise are you clinging to? You, my friend, are not "just a mom." If you have put your faith and trust in Jesus, you are a daughter of the King of Kings and Lord of Lords. You can impact eternity. You can influence a generation. You can leave a legacy by simply being willing for God to use you. Perhaps God is preparing you for something—for such a time as this. Perhaps you are currently in a time of refinement in the desert. But God always keeps His promises. What is your Esther moment? God took an orphan, positioned her in a place of power before the king, and delivered His people. We all can have Esther moments. We are not an accident. The time and place of our existence is not a mistake; it was ordained from the foundations of the earth. We are created for such a time as this! You are a mother for such a time as this!

Chapter 10

PRAYING FOR OUR CHILDREN

I HAVE MEMORIES OF GETTING up early in the mornings as a young girl and going into my parents' bathroom to find my mother kneeling in prayer beside the toilet. You see, while the majority of my life my parents were intentional in their relationship with Jesus and marriage and how they parented us, it didn't start off that way. My very early years of childhood bear a lot of painful memories and scars from my parents being on the brink of divorce. There is a lot of pain that I wish I had never experienced as a young child. When you think your preschooler won't remember you and your spouse fighting, think again. But I am grateful for a mother who prayed.

My parents came really, really close to getting a divorce. My dad will tell you that the only thing that kept him from divorcing my mom was the realization of all he would lose. He didn't want to lose my brother and me. I can assure you, had my parents gotten a divorce, I would be a different person. My foundation and upbringing in a Christian home is why I am who I am today. Had they gone through with the divorce, I can only imagine the kind of trouble I would have gotten into. I would have been bad news. I truly believe that my mom getting up early every single morning to pray for her marriage and family is what saved their marriage. She didn't spend her time talking and complaining to others about her marriage; she spent her time talking to God about her marriage.

Many women who experience what she experienced would have walked out, left, and initiated a divorce. But my mom stayed. She prayed. She was faithful to pray for my dad and my brother and me. Because of her prayers, both of my parents recommitted their lives to Jesus and were re-baptized as a symbol of that change when I was about seven years old. Although far from perfect, from that point on, they were committed to making their marriage the best it could be. They were committed to being intentional in how they parented my brother and me. A marriage was saved and restored because of prayer. I am who I am today because of my mother and father's prayers.

After those early years, I grew up in a home where my parents prayed for my brother and me every single day. They prayed for our future spouses; they prayed for our day at school; they prayed that we would be filled with the knowledge of God's will and that we would bear fruit for His kingdom. Their daily prayer was "We continually ask God to fill you with the knowledge of his will through all the wisdom and understanding that the Spirit gives, so that you may live a life worthy of the Lord and please him in every way: bearing fruit in every good work, growing in the knowledge of God, being strengthened with all power according to his glorious might so that you may have great endurance and patience, and giving joyful thanks to the Father, who has qualified you to share in the inheritance of his holy people in the kingdom of light" (Colossians 1:9b–12). The trajectory of their marriage, my life, and our home changed because of the power of prayer.

There is power in prayer in the name of Jesus!

I believe strongly in the power of prayer. I believe it can absolutely change the direction for any of us in any situation. God hears and answers prayer according to His will! But it is important to note that how God answers may not be the way we would choose for Him to answer the prayers we are praying. This is why it is so important to remember that we are created for His glory and not our own. Our prayers are answered according to how God may receive the glory. They aren't meant to be used for our own self-promotion and gratification.

> Our prayers are answered according to how God may receive the glory. They aren't meant to be used for our own self-promotion and gratification.

One of the hardest things to do as a parent is to understand fully that we are in a spiritual battle in the task of parenthood. It is hard not to take blatant disobedience and disrespect personally. And while we may, in fact, be the target of our child's anger, we must be able to discern what behavior is actually a reflection of the spiritual battle we are facing. I must be able to separate my child's need for Christ and the ways in which it is reflected in the heart, attitude, and actions, all without getting caught up in the drama of that behavior.

Part of the journey we go on as a parent is the emotional roller coaster of a child becoming his or her own person. There is, and should be, a transition of autonomy and independence that takes place with each one of our children. That process isn't always going to look pretty. It can be messy. A child may question authority. They may begin to question the foundation on which we have raised them. They may even question their faith. We want our children to move from a place of obeying just "because I said so" to a place of owning what they believe.

Our job as moms is to point our children to Jesus, giving them a firm foundation with a biblical worldview. But when we remember that this is a spiritual battle we are facing, we realize that we are not alone in this fight. I have to learn not to take things personally. I have to remember that my fight and my struggle reaching my child's heart is described in Ephesians 6:12, "For our struggle is not against flesh and blood, but against the rulers, against the authorities, against the powers of this dark world and against the spiritual forces of evil in the heavenly realms." We are in a spiritual battle as parents.

If we are going to engage in the battle, then we must be fully armed and ready to fight. We must first understand and acknowledge we are at war and know who we are fighting. We are taught in Scripture (Ephesians 6:11–18) not only who is the enemy, as referenced above, but also how to arm ourselves for spiritual warfare. "Put on the full armor of God, so that you can take your stand against the devil's schemes" (v. 11). God is very clear that we must understand that our husband, children, neighbors, co-workers are not the enemy. We are in the midst of spiritual warfare and are fighting against the devil and spiritual forces of the evil one.

The Bible goes on to teach us step by step how to arm ourselves for this kind of spiritual warfare. "Therefore put on the full armor of God, so that when the day of evil comes, you may be able to stand your ground, and after you have done everything, to stand. Stand firm then, with the belt of truth buckled around your waist, with the breastplate of righteousness in place, and with your feet fitted with the readiness that comes from the gospel of peace. In addition to all this, take up the shield of faith, with which you can extinguish all the flaming arrows of the evil one. Take the helmet of salvation and the sword of the Spirit, which is the word of God" (vv. 13-17). We are clearly instructed to walk in truth and honesty at all times and to live a life of obedience and righteousness, being right with God. We must know the Word of God in order to discern what is truth while living a life that reflects Jesus, sharing the peace and love that He offers to a lost and dying world.

Additionally, we must be able to live from a place of walking by faith and not by sight. There is too much evil in this world, and if we get caught up with what we see, we will become discouraged and hopeless. Instead, we must live life from a place of faith, understanding that we are in spiritual warfare.

Finally, Scripture continues with this very important admonition, "And pray in the Spirit on all occasions with all kinds of prayers and requests. With this in mind, be alert and always keep on praying for all the Lord's people" (v. 18). After we are told who we are fighting and how we should prepare for battle, then we are instructed with this command to pray always. This is not optional or a suggestion. This is a command from the Lord Jesus. Our enemy is the devil. Our uniform is knowing the Word of God and walking in truth,

> This is how we win the battle: on our knees in prayer.

righteousness, and faith, having the Word of God hidden in our hearts so that we can discern how to fight each battle, and owning the fact that we are sons and daughters of the King of Kings and Lord of Lords. But then God very clearly tells us to pray. This is how we win the battle: on our knees in prayer. This is how we do spiritual warfare.

Mothers, we must know the Word of God so that we can teach it to our children. We must put on the full armor of God so we can be prepared to fight the battle we are in. And finally, we must fully understand how that battle is fought—on our knees in prayer. The battle is way too big for us without God on our side. Our spiritual eyes must be opened. When we begin seeing life through a spiritual lens, we will see the world and all that is occurring from a different vantage point. Armed with the power of God through prayer, we will begin to live and move from a place of faith and trust in God. We will live our lives in confidence.

Additionally, we must begin teaching our children to pray. We need to teach them how to put on the armor of God and engage in spiritual warfare by hitting their knees in prayer. Our children need to see us leading by example. Unfortunately, we are not praying in all occasions. We are not asking God for wisdom, as He teaches us to do. We are not praying that we will be given words from God to fearlessly proclaim the gospel. In fact, in our own homes, with our own kids, we are intimidated to speak God's truths. We are not praying that we will have the words directly from God to know how to handle each and every situation we face as mothers. We are not praying that we will have a quick and ready answer from God to boldly proclaim His truth to our children. And the reality is, all too often, we don't have this ready answer because 1) we aren't asking God to give us an answer and 2) we don't know the Word of God ourselves. I love how simply my friend and mentor, Dr. David Vanderpoel, puts it, "You can't teach what you don't know."

Our goal should be that each one of our children individually would own their faith and relationship with Jesus and that they too would put on the full armor of God to fight the spiritual battle with us. Although the parenting process begins as a struggle to reach our child's heart, eventually we want our child to own his or her own faith and join forces with us in this battle. We want to move to the same side, the same team. We want our child to see that the struggle is a spiritual battle. We are in a spiritual warfare. We want them to take up the shield of faith when defending their faith to others. We want them to own that belt of truth when challenged to be forthcoming with honesty or deception. We want them to know the Word of God so that they can use that power as the sword of the Spirit in defense against peer pressure.

> "You can't teach what you don't know."

My teenager is not my enemy. My fight is not against flesh and blood. We must understand that our kids are not the enemy. We also must be fully armed for battle. All too often, moms, we try to fight this battle unarmed. We try to take a battle on that we aren't prepared or even able to fight. We try to own something that isn't ours to own. We wake up each morning and are "naked," feeling like we are personally being attacked when the reality is that we have no idea who we are really in war against.

It's not a personal attack. Our children are not the enemy! Satan, the father of lies, is the enemy. John 10:10 tell us, "The thief comes only to steal and kill and destroy; I have come that they may have life, and have it to the full."

Moms, we are entering the battlefield of parenting completely unprepared and totally unarmed. We start the parenting journey without knowing that we are entering a war zone. There is a reason that our culture has abandoned the virtue and high calling of motherhood. Mothers have forgotten that this is a spiritual battle, and Satan is winning against our families.

Mothers, I urge you and challenge you to understand that you are engaged in spiritual warfare. War is being waged against your marriages and children. Your family is a prime battleground for the enemy. And it's because we as Christians don't fully understand and embrace the fact that marriage is a covenant relationship from God that we aren't fighting to protect it. God instituted the family. Satan wants to destroy it. And we are letting him.

> God instituted the family. Satan wants to destroy it. And we are letting him.

The covenant of marriage is a beautiful picture of Christ and the church. Our marriages should honor Christ in the way that we love and serve one another in marriage. It is through the covenant of marriage that God gives us a tangible picture of what the relationship between us as believers and Jesus should look like. This is why marriage is sacred and holy. While our culture has forsaken the respect and honor of traditional marriage, it's still holy in God's eyes. Once again, we go against culture and society when we fight to protect and preserve our marriages. Our marriages are an opportunity to be a picture to others of Christ's love and forgiveness. Marriage is made up of two sinners living under the same roof. When we forgive one another and show God's grace and mercy in our marriage relationship, we have an opportunity to be a tangible picture of what Christ offers to mankind. And best of all, our marriage can and should give our children an up close and personal look at that sacrificial love that God gave us through Jesus. Our marriages show our children firsthand the love, forgiveness, and grace that Christ extends to us.

Marriages and families are falling apart because we aren't fighting for them. We are entering into these holy and sacred covenants without a knowledge of the sacred meaning of marriage and how to fight for our children in parenting. It is no wonder that something so important to God, which has an opportunity to tell His love story for mankind, is under attack. It is not surprising that Satan wants to rip apart this tangible picture of God's redeeming love. Our culture represents the depravity of man and our turning our backs on God. Satan doesn't want our marriages to succeed. He doesn't want the family to be a spiritual picture of the fruit of a godly relationship. Satan is after our marriages and after our children. We must be vigilant to fight for both.

Spiritual warfare is fought on our knees in prayer. Not only are we failing to put on the armor of God to face this battle for our marriages and kids, but we are also failing to pray daily. Culture tells us to buy more stuff, enroll in more activities, and stay busy. God tells us to slow down, drop to our knees, and spend time with Him. But Satan is perfectly happy with our busy lifestyles because it means that we are too busy to pray. It should be absolutely no surprise that our culture does not value marriage. It shouldn't surprise us that marriages, even in the church, are falling apart. It shouldn't surprise us that children are rebellious and uninterested in God. We have been fighting the battle all wrong. We aren't prepared.

My husband and girls absolutely love Marvel movies. They love all of the superheroes: the conflict of good versus evil and the struggle between light and dark. The idea that there is a hero and a villain is exhilarating. So, as every new Marvel movie comes out, my girls anxiously await its arrival. They will watch these movies over and over again, never growing tired of the almost-predictable conflict between the hero and villain. The villain is always out to destroy the world, and the hero always swoops in to save the day. Everyone loves a good story of good versus evil, and we all love it when the hero wins. We create these stories in many different forms, through books, magazines, movies, and games. This make-believe world allows us to live vicariously through the fantasy, enjoying a good fight to the death for a cause that we morally believe is right and true.

And yet, the world we live in is much like a superhero movie. There is spiritual warfare taking place every day. There is an actual battle between good and evil, and we need to know which side we are on. Who are we fighting for? We know how the story will end. God wins. We can rest in this confidence. The exciting part is that we can play a vital role on this earth as we drop to our knees in prayer and allow the Holy Spirit to fight on our behalf. The power of prayer equips us to battle the flaming darts that the enemy aims at our homes, our marriages, and our children.

We have the answer at our fingertips, and yet sometimes we just want to roll over and play dead instead of getting up to fight. We choose not to take the time to pray. We say that we are too busy. In actuality, however, we are too busy not to pray. Raising our children is a demanding task. It requires so much of our time, energy, and attention. As such, we are in a constant state of need for prayer.

While I do have dedicated time on my knees in prayer while my husband is at work and my kids are in school, I find myself seeking God's counsel and aid 24/7. I am praying in the car, on a walk, going into the grocery store. Prayer is a relationship. Prayer is communications with God. I don't have to set up an appointment to talk to my best friend or husband. I just talk to them. The same is true of God. He is our Father, and we can approach Him anytime and anywhere. While deliberately setting aside time for prayer is imperative and valuable, I don't have to rely on that alone. Prayer is an on-going conversation with our Heavenly Father who wants to know us and love us and support us in our roles as mothers.

Before our children were born, we began praying for them while they were still growing in my womb. Every night to this day, my husband and I pray for our girls. I lay my hands on them and pray that they would have dreams and visions from God even as they sleep. I pray that God would set them apart for His purposes and use them for His glory. I pray that they would know Him. I pray for their future spouses. I pray that He will bring them each a godly husband in His timing. I often imagine what ages those boys are and pray for them in this current stage. I pray for the boys' parents, that they will have wisdom as they rear their boys. I pray for the marriages of the moms and dads of each of these boys, that they would be strong and stay together. I pray for those boys and our daughters to keep them-selves pure and set apart for all that God has in store for them. I am proclaiming my faith that God has great plans in store for my girls' futures. Then we hug and kiss them and speak a verse of Scripture over them from the Old Testament: "The Lord bless you and keep you; the Lord make his face shine on you and be gracious to you; the Lord turn his face toward you and give you peace" (Numbers 6:24–26). I love this blessing! I speak it over each one of our daughters nightly, blessing them with this truth and promise.

God used dreams and visions all throughout the Bible. As my girls sleep, I want them to hear from God. I myself want to learn to hear His voice all the day long, whether waking or dreaming. Obviously, we hear from God as we read His Word and when we spend time in prayer, but I also believe that God can speak to us while we sleep. So from our girls' early years, I have prayed that God would be present in their slumber and speak to them through their dreams.

Our two oldest daughters asked Jesus into their lives on January 17, 2006. I had been reading them a book about God's love for us and the gift of His Son Jesus. When we finished reading, Reagan, age four and a half, and Jordan, age two and a half, said that they believed that Jesus had died for them, and both said they wanted to ask Jesus to come into their lives.

With a great boldness, Reagan said she wanted to take Jordan upstairs to pray alone to ask Jesus to come into their lives. You see, Reagan was very familiar with the passage in Matthew 6:6a that says, "But when you pray, go into your room, close the door and pray to your Father, who is unseen." Both of the girls would spend every afternoon listening to the Bible on CD while they played, and they had memorized a great deal of Scripture. So Reagan wanted the two of them to be alone in her walk-in closet when they asked Jesus into their hearts. The two of them went off. When they came back downstairs, of course I wanted to make sure that they understood what asking Jesus into their lives really meant since they were so young. Oh, the faith of a child! I began going over the details of salvation: what it meant for God to send His Son to be our sacrifice so that we can have access to God and the fact that Jesus rose from the grave and we can have the Holy Spirit in our lives always. Then I prayed with each of them and had them pray out loud with me, asking Jesus to come into their lives.

Shortly after Reagan had asked Jesus into her heart, she wanted to be baptized as a testimony of her relationship with Jesus. Jordan was adamant that she was not interested in baptism. And, of course, we weren't going to push it. The relationship with Jesus has to be personal. The Holy Spirit will prompt when He is ready. And so Reagan was baptized, but we dropped the subject with Jordan. It would come up from time to time, with Jordan always making it extremely clear that she was not interested.

But, as I said, I believe in the power of prayer and God's use of dreams and visions. Late one Sunday afternoon when Jordan was five years old, our family was driving to a friend's house. Like every other car ride, the conversation was all over the map. About thirty minutes into the trip, Jordan announces out of nowhere and with authority, "I need to get baptized." Now, mind you, we had not even been talking about baptism. It was not a recent conversation by any means. This announcement took us completely by surprise. And

Jordan said it with such confidence and authority that we were quite frankly shocked.

"You do?" I asked. "Why?"

Without hesitation, Jordan said, "I had a dream last night that I got baptized, and I know that God is telling me to be baptized."

Where in the world was this coming from? I had to focus to stay on the road while I was driving! Yes, I reassured myself, my little girl just calmly announced that God had spoken to her in a dream and told her that she needed to be baptized. We had stopped talking about baptism months before, but this five-year-old girl, with child-like faith, had a dream. She was ready. God had spoken to her even while she slept.

God cares about everything in our lives! God should be the first resource we go to for any need, any struggle, any praise.

> God should be the first resource we go to for any need, any struggle, any praise.

Too often, our first response is to call a friend with our fears or concerns or to post our good news or latest crisis on Facebook. This often leads us to spend more time talking about the problem and the need for prayer than actually praying. Instead, our first response should be to talk to God. Our Father God—our Abba, our Daddy—is the perfect parent and knows what is best. He can fight on our behalf.

When we feel exhausted and overwhelmed, we need to pray. When our children are struggling with friendships, that's an opportunity for us to pray. When our family dynamics seem unsteady, we need to pray. When our kids are struggling with a new concept in school or when academics just seem too hard, we should pray. Every time we get in the car to drive, we should pray for protection that we won't hit anyone and no one will hit us. We should pray that God would place a hedge of protection around our family (Job 1:10). We should pray that we have favor at work. We should pray for a parking space to open for us at the mall or grocery store. We should pray for wisdom in navigating relationships, or how to handle our child's attitudes and behaviors. We should pray that God would go before difficult situations and soften hearts and prepare the way going before us. This should be our first response—our lifeline.

Last winter, we spent Christmas at Walt Disney World. We were to fly back home on December 30th to make it home before New Year's Eve. Then we received a text that our flights were delayed and a cancellation looked increasingly likely. Due to severe weather across different parts of the United States, all air travel was severely delayed or cancelled, and the ripple effect was only increasing the length of the delays and cancellations. Our luggage had already been sent to the airport. We were spending the afternoon at Downtown Disney on the phone trying to come up with an alternate game plan. Todd was on his phone unsuccessfully trying to find a hotel room for us to stay in an additional night due to the cancellations, while I was on my phone with the airline trying to rebook our flights.

As I looked up from taking notes on my conversation with the airline, I noticed our three girls sitting tightly together in a circle on the curb, holding hands and praying right in the middle of Downtown Disney. When I got off the phone, I asked them what they were doing. They answered they were just asking Jesus to sort out all the airline troubles so we could make it home that evening. Well, wouldn't you know we were notified by the airlines that while our flight had been delayed, they were still able to get all five of us out on a flight that evening only a couple hours after the original departure was scheduled. God cares about every detail of our lives!

Prayer can also be an opportunity to share God's good news with others. We are all aware of the story in the Bible of Daniel praying three times a day. Now Daniel had already seen his friends Shadrach, Meshach, and Abednego delivered from the fiery furnace. Because they would not bow down and worship the king but would only worship the one true God, their punishment was to be thrown into a furnace of fire. God showed up and delivered them. They were not even burned (Daniel 3). Later in the book of Daniel, when a decree goes out ordering Daniel to stop praying, he refuses. Daniel had already seen God show up in a big way with his friends. Daniel knew and believed in the power of prayer and was not going to stop this conversation with God. His penalty was to be thrown into a lions' den. Once again, God shows up and closes the lions' mouths so that Daniel escapes without even a scratch (Daniel 6). Not only had Daniel seen God show up in miraculous ways sparing his life and his friends' lives, he was now able to have a voice and place of influence when the king noticed something different about Daniel. The king ordered for everyone to worship the one true God, the God of Daniel.

A couple of years ago, our family spent some time in London. One afternoon after a day spent walking the streets of the city, we went into a local cafe for afternoon tea. We ordered a variety of hot teas, sandwiches, and scones. Upon receiving our order, we held hands to pray as a family. Our waiter had walked by and, after waiting for us to finish praying, made comment that he had never in all his years seen a family pray together. He was almost in tears. He told us that in

London that was never seen. You may occasionally see a Catholic bow and make the sign of the cross on a rare occurrence, he told us, but never had he seen anyone actually pray—especially not as a family.

This opened a door for conversation. We briefly acknowledged that we always take time to pray and thank God for our meal when we eat. At the conclusion of our afternoon tea, as we were leaving the cafe, my husband went and found the waiter and told him about a local church we knew of in the area. Todd encouraged him to go visit it and learn more about Jesus. He wrote down the name of the church and told him to go check it out for himself. While a very brief encounter, this time of prayer as a family offered a window of sharing Jesus with a man who was searching for hope and meaning in life.

The story of Daniel also reminds us of the power of a prayer life. If God spoke the mountains into existence, then God can move the mountains. God can close the mouths of lions. God can prevent us from getting burned. God is a God of the impossible. This is super exciting! Remember, God is our Father. We are His children, and we have direct access to Him on behalf of our own children. How could we not be excited about that? And yet, we choose not to exercise that privilege we have as sons and daughters of the Creator of the universe! How could I not want to talk to God? The idea that God can do the impossible and that I can live my life watching the supernatural play out in the natural gets me excited! The power of prayer is where it's at!

When we move into a place of prayer for our children, we aren't fighting this battle alone. We have God Almighty on our side fighting for us. When I try to fight alone, I quickly feel overwhelmed and defeated before I ever make it out of bed. It feels like the weight is too much to carry. But we don't have to carry the burden alone. We don't have to fight the battle alone. The Holy Spirit is on our side ready to fight for us.

> Culture says post your problems on Facebook or call a friend, but God says, "Come to me. The battle is mine."

Marriage is a spiritual battle. Parenting is a spiritual battle. We must begin to see these battles for what they are with our spiritual eyes. The battle is fought on our knees in prayer. Again, this is countercultural. Culture says post your problems on Facebook or call a friend, but God says, "Come to me. The battle is mine."

There is power in the name of Jesus!

Chapter 11

REACHING OUR CHILD'S HEART

ONE HOT TEXAS SUMMER AFTERNOON when I was still in college, I was driving a couple of children that I was watching for the afternoon to a nearby park to play. As we were making our way down the road, the three-year-old hit his baby sister when she grabbed a toy from him. She was the innocent baby who thought she was joining in his fun. He was the big brother who didn't like his action figure being grabbed out of his hands. He reacted like most kids do in frustration and hit his little sister to make his disapproval known. He screamed. She screamed.

There was little I could do while I was driving. When we arrived at the park, I helped get this little three-year-old out of his car seat. I took him by the hand, and kneeling down on eye level, I asked him what he had done wrong. He repeated back to me the incident that had occurred. With remorse in his eyes, he said he was sorry.

Typically, there would be a consequence for this kind of disobedience. But, I also knew there was a teachable opportunity here. I looked him in the eyes and said, "What you did was wrong, but I am going to have grace on you and not give you a consequence this time." He thought about it for a minute, and with all sincerity, he asked, "How long will Grace have to sit on me?" You see, Grace was his little sister's name! He thought that I was going to make Grace sit on him! Completely caught off guard, I laughed and explained that what I meant by "grace" was God's mercy to us when we sin but don't get what we deserve. So, that afternoon included a teachable moment for me, as well: Young children are very concrete, and we need to be sure that we clearly communicate what is important.

The most significant lesson from that afternoon, however, was the importance of grace in our parenting. We parent out of what we know and what was modeled for us. Unfortunately, that isn't always a good thing. Even the best of families are not perfect. We parent from a place of sin. Reaching our child's heart for Jesus is a challenge, as we are continually reminded of our own weakness and sin nature. Not only do we need to be willing to show grace to our own children, but we as parents also need God's grace.

At many of my speaking engagements, moms are quick to confess that yelling is a real struggle for them. Often, yelling was modeled for us by our own parents. If yelling was the way you were parented, chances are you will yell at your kids because that is what you know. Whether you like it or not, it has become a habit, or your "normal." Yelling—or, let's take it a step further, anger—comes from a place of not being in control. When we yell or get angry, there is often something else going on that has pushed us to take our frustrations out on others.

Let's say you have asked your kids to get their shoes on so that they can go to the grocery store with you. You come back five minutes later with your keys and are ready to walk out the door. The kids are still sitting on the couch, watching TV and obviously disobeying. This kind of situation creates in us a feeling of being ignored, which can lead to us yelling as an expression of our frustration. We feel out of control. Possibly our response has very little to do with our kids and more to do with other stresses in our life. Maybe you just got off a phone call regarding an overdue bill that you don't have the money to pay. Your children's lack of obedience just creates another sense of being out of control, and your yelling comes from your own place of frustration.

While our external stress does not excuse our children's disobedience, we must become accountable in how we respond to reaching our child's heart during times of disobedience and sinning. We must first pause and respond not from a place of anger but a place of teaching—calling our children to account for their actions and behaviors. We are all human. We all sin. We all get frustrated. But we are called to something greater. As the Bible reminds us in Ephesians 4:26a, "In your anger, do not sin." We have the opportunity to model biblical anger and frustration for our children. When our children disobey, our job is to be in control of our own words, actions, and behaviors so that we can call our children to obedience without sinning ourselves. Trust me—it's hard. Like I said, we are not perfect parents.

We have the opportunity in these moments to show our kids the fatherly heart of God by responding to disobedience without losing our temper. But let's say we do lose control of our emotions and sin in our anger—what an excellent opportunity to let our children know that we are sinners in need of forgiveness and grace too! When this occurs, we must be willing to humble ourselves and ask our children to forgive us. We should pray together and seek God's forgiveness as well. Our children show us so much grace when we mess up. As a family, we should always make it a practice to embrace every honest confession and to acknowledge the humility of each repentant heart.

When our goal in parenting is reaching our children's hearts for Jesus and making them aware of their sin and need for a Savior, we can turn everything into a teachable moment. We want to be proactive in our parenting, not reactive. We want to create an atmosphere in which we are sharing the gospel daily with our children. We want our homes to be a place that reflects God's redemptive story at every turn. When a mistake is made, we have the opportunity to share the grace, love, and forgiveness that Jesus has to offer. We need to be at a constant place of being in the presence of Jesus. We want to see our children not just learning head knowledge about Jesus but living in the presence of Jesus and knowing Him in a real and personal way. Our homes should reflect this constant state of experiencing the presence of Jesus and living out the gospel.

Moms, we also need to forgive ourselves when we mess up. This is where it is important to parent with no regrets! We acknowledge that mistakes will be part of parenting, but they won't define us. We are not perfect. We are sinful parents who parent from a place of imperfection. Women can be our own worst critics. We can be so hard on ourselves when we don't feel worthy or good enough when mistakes are made. If we live in regrets, we will be paralyzed by our fear. We will teach our children that forgiveness isn't real—that it's not sufficient. My friend, God's grace and forgiveness are always sufficient! Rather than role-modeling bondage from past mistakes, we must learn how to live in freedom from the past.

When our children were very young and needed to be disciplined, Todd and I would make it part of our practice to hold them and pray with them, asking for God's forgiveness of their disobedience. A very important part of discipline is discipleship. Discipline is necessary to keep our children safe and instruct them in the basic principles of right and wrong. But the practice of discipleship involves helping our children build a firm foundation based on God's Word. It is our standard for a biblical worldview. Disobedience—sin—has consequences. When we move into a place of discipleship, we teach our children why sin has consequences and also the principles of blessings and curses and forgiveness. We help them establish a worldview that is founded on the gospel, and we continue to use our homes to share the redemptive story of the gospel.

Even through tears of discipline, the subsequent opportunities for discipleship always provided a sweet time for restoration for our family. It gave us an opportunity to tell our children that, yes, we all disobey and make wrong choices, and, yes, those choices do have consequences. But we also had the opportunity to share the good news that with sin we can experience forgiveness because of Jesus. We would pray with our girls, asking God to forgive them for their disobedience and help them make things right with whomever they offended. We always hugged them and kissed them and reminded them that when we ask God to forgive us, we are forgiven—we can move on. Additionally, once our children came to a personal relationship with Jesus, we encouraged them to take even more responsibility to pray and ask the Holy Spirit to help them obey and make wiser choices in the future. This takes a lot of pressure off us as parents when our children respond directly to the Holy Spirit and His conviction.

When our goal is reaching our children's hearts for Jesus, we teach them that their attitudes and behaviors are either showing the love of Jesus or they are not. As they experience the gospel, they should be sharing the gospel, living it out for the world to see God's great love story for humanity. One of the verses we had our children memorize when they were two years old was "Even small children are known by their actions" (Proverbs 20:11a). We wanted our girls to understand that their actions send messages to others. If they are fighting with one another or not sharing, they are not showing the love of Jesus. We would have them say this verse before we would go to a friend's house or have a playdate because we wanted to remind them that everything we say and do reflects our hearts and can show the love of Jesus to others. The old adage, "Actions speak louder than words" is true even for children. So we have an opportunity for our attitudes and behaviors to show others the redemptive love of Jesus and God's grace. Parenting can be an example to a lost and dying world as we share the love, grace, and forgiveness that are available to all of us when we trust Christ with our lives. Our children's attitudes and behaviors become an opportunity to reflect God's redemptive love story to those watching our family from afar.

> So we have an opportunity for our attitudes and behaviors to show others the redemptive love of Jesus and God's grace.

"What is your A verse?" I would ask my three girls when they were very young. "What is your B verse?" and on we would go through the alphabet, with a corresponding verse to match each letter. This is still

> If you can talk, you can memorize Scripture.

a common question in our home today. My philosophy has always been "if you can talk, you can memorize Scripture." Children are like little sponges! They absorb everything you tell them and they want to learn. When they are young, we have such an amazing opportunity to teach our children the Word of God. So in our house, if you can talk, you are memorizing Scripture. We started with small verses. But we were always intentional with the verses we chose so that they could apply God's wisdom with daily practical examples.

When we are intentional in reaching our child's heart for God, we want to make sure we are using His Word as our foundation for teaching. Scripture memorization was the best teaching tool I had in my toolkit! For example, when one of our daughters chose not to obey or did not obey immediately or with a good attitude, we would ask them, "What is your C verse?" Ephesians 6:1 says, "Children obey your parents in the Lord for this is right." The best part of parenting with Scripture is that the Holy Spirit convicts our children's hearts and calls them to obedience for us. We don't get into a power struggle. I don't have to get upset or raise my voice. I simply ask them to quote Scripture. The Holy Spirit and God's Word are on my side, convicting and calling our children to accountability.

Remember, obedience is a heart issue. If our attitudes don't reflect a cheerful heart, then we are not really obeying. We may be going through the act or going through the motions, but that is not real obedience. Parenting is all about the heart. We have got to reach the heart. We must help our children become aware that they are born sinners in need of a Savior. We need a heart transplant. We have to reach the foundation of the heart, not just acquiring the action or behavior.

Our children can become quite skilled with the act of going through the motions and pretending to obey, all while their heart is far from obedience. Teenagers are really good at this. Have you ever been in a classroom with teenagers? You give them a task, and, begrudgingly, they roll their eyes and make a lame effort to do what you have asked. They think it's funny and cool to make obedience difficult for authority. But, in reality, it is a reflection of their heart. I can walk into any classroom and know immediately which students have a heart of obedience and whose parents are doing the hard work at home to provide that foundational teaching. I can also know immediately whose parents are not requiring obedience or have given up. Additionally, it is just as easy to spot those who are deceitful, manipulating the truth just enough to avoid getting caught. Our actions always reflect the heart.

What about when our children get upset and frustrated with their friends, classmates, or siblings? "A soft answer turns away wrath" (Proverbs 15:1a ESV). We can help our children understand that provoking others or having an angry response won't help the situation. When we reply with gentleness, we help prevent stirring others to anger.

But our all-time favorite verse is our D verse. "Do EVERYTHING without grumbling or arguing" (Philippians 2:14, emphasis mine). No complaining! We are seeking hearts of obedience without complaining and arguing about walking in obedience. True obedience is done immediately and cheerfully. This was, and continues to be, the verse most often used in our home.

Riley, our youngest daughter, has always been our pickiest eater. Although a good eater, she is the one who has been the biggest challenge when it comes to eating. She would prefer to eat peanut butter and chocolate on any given day for any given meal. While we do want our children to have their own likes and dislikes when it comes to food, we also expect them to eat a nutritious, well-balanced diet so that their little bodies can grow strong. It is my job to teach them about nutrition and to do what I can to give them a healthy lifestyle. And so, saying our D verse around dinnertime became a common occurrence as Riley looked begrudgingly at her spinach. Sometimes, we have to do what we don't like doing, but we always have a choice in the attitude in which it is done. Teaching our children the Word of God allows their hearts to become aware of God's authority and His principles for living.

> Teaching our children the Word of God allows their hearts to become aware of God's authority and His principles for living.

As my father often said, "Rules without a relationship lead to rebellion." What we want to create for our children is a relationship with Jesus—not legalism, not rules, but a relationship. I want my girls to know Jesus, to have a relationship with Him and not to get caught up with the legalism of doing acts for performance. Life should be fun in the process of learning. It is not about being serious and boring. Who wants to do life without fun? If we're just making rules for our kids to obey and we aren't making our Christian life fun and inviting, of course, they aren't going to want this kind of life. Getting creative and making it fun to learn about God and His Word is how we should approach parenting. Legalism has got to go! We need to get rid of the legalism and enjoy life, all while creating an atmosphere of capturing our child's heart for God. Legalism and rules will always lead to rebellion. Reaching our child's heart is about a relationship with Jesus.

As our children began to read on their own, we encouraged them to have their own time of fellowship with Jesus, praying and studying His Word. I really don't care what that looks like for each of them, as long as they are spending time with Jesus and are reading the Word of God. Because all three of my daughters have very different personalities, it looks different for each of them. One likes to keep a spiritual journal to write down what she is learning about God. Another enjoys doing a verse-by-verse study of a book of the Bible. My middle daughter, Jordan, is very artsy. Being able to put anything to music helps her learn. She listens to a lot of praise and worship music while reading the Bible because that helps her process how God loves her. So how our girls spend time reading the Bible, memorizing Scripture, and praying is up to them, but we encourage them to do it.

Thankfully, because it has been a part of their upbringing and because they personally want to grow in their relationship with Jesus, this time of fellowship is not a chore or something they resent. They look forward to it and enjoy it. They love sharing how they spent their time with Jesus and what they are learning. But, again, encouraging them to build a relationship with Jesus individually is the goal. It is not about any set of rules that govern how they spend their time with Him, what time of day it occurs, or how long it lasts, but rather, it's about the relationship itself.

In their self-righteous behavior, the legalistic Pharisees looked down on others when things weren't done a certain way. We, as moms, do not want to become like Pharisees and look down on others in the parenting of their children. We also don't want to be legalistic or pharisaical in how we introduce our own children to Jesus. In our humble desire to reach our children's hearts for Jesus, we must encourage one another as iron sharpens iron. Instead of becoming pious and self-righteous, we should become known by our love as we support and encourage one another.

In the process of reaching our children's hearts for Jesus, we want them to begin truly owning their faith and personal relationship with Jesus—making it their own. I was listening to a podcast several months ago as a pastor described an incident involving a former pastor who had committed a terrible sin against several members of the congregation. As his family dealt with the aftermath of this scandal coming to light, the current pastor told his son, "Son, I hope this doesn't affect your faith." I love the son's response to his father: "That's not going to happen, Dad, because I have had my own personal encounter with who Jesus is."

Our children's faith will be challenged. Their faith may be put to the test at school or one day in the workplace. Some may have to pay the ultimate price for their faith. But even if we are not called to die for our faith, we all will experience difficult things. In order to completely own our faith—even to the point of being willing to die for what we believe—we must have a personal encounter with Jesus.

Although we are imperfect parents, pointing our children to God allows them to see their perfect Heavenly Father, who is full of forgiveness, grace, mercy, justice, kindness, and wisdom. We want our children to see Jesus and the father heart of God despite our own weakness, sin, and imperfection. This becomes our ultimate game plan in our parenting—reaching our children's hearts for Jesus. We must make it our mission to point our children to Christ and their need for Him. Our homes are a place to share God's great love story at every turn. Our marriages, our parenting, and our families are all a beautiful picture of the redemptive story of the gospel.

Chapter 12

FREEDOM FROM FEAR

MY GREATEST FEAR IN BECOMING a mother was not losing a child but, instead, leaving a child. My senior year at Baylor, one of my close friends lost her battle with breast cancer, leaving behind her five precious children. I took care of these children, ages eight and under, for an entire year. I homeschooled and cared for them while finishing up my senior year of college, until their father remarried a phenomenal young lady. I like to consider them my first five children! I loved them as my own.

My friend's death affected me so greatly that I was paralyzed by the fear of dying as a young mother. I was again faced with the reality of what happens at death, and I had to come to terms with if I was prepared to die. My faith was tested, and I had to decide if what I believed was really true. I didn't want what happened to my friend to happen to me. I didn't want my children to lose a mother. I was sure no one would love them like I loved them. No one would care for them the way I could. I honestly didn't trust that anyone would be good enough for them and their care. I wanted to protect them.

But what bothered me the most, and why I would cry myself to sleep at night, was the thought of the pain that my children would endure if they lost their mother. When I lost my friend, I was there to take care of her children every day that first year. Watching them grieve absolutely broke my heart and truly scarred me, going into motherhood. I didn't ever want to leave my children; I didn't ever want them to endure the pain of that kind of loss. I was not in control if I wasn't there to comfort them. I wanted control. I didn't want my children to have to suffer or be sad or angry if I were gone. I was scared to die.

I was consumed by fear, and I couldn't keep living this way. I had always been a "live life to the fullest" kind of girl, and now I was more consumed with "what if" questions and the fear of risk. I had always made it a point to live life with no regrets, to seize the day, take risk, and do the impossible. But once I brought children into world, I became almost paralyzed by the fear of needing to play it safe. I needed to ensure that no one got hurt.

Of course, kids are resilient, but it was still a long and painful journey for this young family—and for me. Now my friend's children are grown, some with children of their own, but I still like to think of them as my first five sons and daughters. And what a blessing it was to introduce my own three daughters to some of them! I absolutely love that one of them told my girls, "I was your mom's first daughter to love." My girls beamed with pride, feeling like they had just gained another sister! Those five precious children have had a huge and lasting impact on my life. I love them so much.

We were recently at one of Riley's soccer games, and I saw a young girl fall to the ground when the ball barreled into her stomach. The father, immediately and without thinking, ran out onto the field to grab his daughter to check on her. Although she brushed off the fall, not thinking anything of it, you could still hear him confessing later that it was his job as the father to ensure his daughter was okay. It wasn't the coach's job or the team's job; it was his job. As parents, we will do anything to protect our children and keep them from pain. What parent doesn't? I think this is natural for all parents. We innately want to protect our young, and we will risk everything to keep them from harm.

My fear of death in my early years as a mother was all consuming. It was paralyzing. Something had to change. I would pray and have others pray for me. Still, it felt like the fear would never leave. There was a heaviness, a bondage to fear that consumed me. Then one day there was a breakthrough. It was like the chains of fear were gone. Literally, I felt freedom. It was a bondage that I could actually feel leave. It was a miracle! I had begun learning about the sovereignty of God and fully trusting that He is in control. I finally understood the passage in Matthew 6:27 that says, "Can any one of you by worrying add a single hour to your life?" Our days are already numbered. God knew in advance when I was going to be born, and He knows the day and hour when I will take my last breath. It is not going to catch the God of the universe by surprise. My life is in His hands. My husband's life is in His hands. My daughters' lives are in His hands.

Out of the fear of dying, I was not fully living. Fear consumed me, but when I was finally set free from this bondage, I was completely at peace. I began to understand that God is sovereign. I began to believe that God is good all the time—even when bad things happen. I began to trust God when I couldn't be in control. Then I began to actively turn over what little control I did have and trusted Him with my life, my husband, and my girls. I was now willingly offering Him any control I claimed to have and turning over everything in my life to Him. My husband is His. My children are His. My life is His. Whether we live or die, we are in His hands. Fear was gone!

This absolutely revolutionized the way that I began living out my life. I was suddenly no longer afraid to die. I began to live life with a newfound freedom. I began to fully understand that my life is in God's hands. I didn't have to hold on so tightly out of fear of losing control. I could rest in the freedom that God is bigger than all my fears. If He can speak the world into being, surely He can handle the activities of my day. If He created me, He controls my days. If He entrusted me with the care of my daughters, they are His gift to me, and He loves them more than I ever could, then I can trust Him to care for them. My focus shifted.

I began to realize that I had been in bondage to fear. And fear is not of God. Fear is from the enemy, Satan. I had allowed my mind to be consumed by something that was not of God. It affected the way that I was parenting and greatly inhibited my ability to be the mother that I needed to be. I didn't have to live my life in fear. While I don't want to die, I'm also not afraid to die. This freedom gave me a whole new perspective on life and how I parented my girls. It did two things. First, it freed me from my personal fear of death; and second, it allowed me to trust the sovereignty of

As a child of God, I don't have to live in fear.

God with my life and the lives of my children. As a child of God, I don't have to live in fear.

I fully surrendered to the fact that I am not in control, but God is. I can't add even another minute to my life, no matter how hard I try. He controls my life and is the author of my life. He knows how long I will live, so I don't have to worry about it. He knows how long each one of my girls will live. I can rest in that. I can rest in the fact that because my faith is in Jesus, I will be with Him forever in eternity. Life continues after death. I can rest in the fact that each one of my three princesses have their own personal relationship with Jesus and regardless of when they leave this earth, they will be in the presence of their Father when they die and live with Him forever. It is human nature to try to hold on and grip a little tighter the things we fear or the things we can't control. But I found more freedom when I was able to loosen the grip and let go. Not being in control never felt so good.

Fear is a real struggle for moms. While other moms may not struggle with the fear of dying as I did, many moms are often paralyzed by different anxieties. Whether it is the fear of strangers, the fear of accidents, the fear of all the violence in the world we live in, or the fear of not doing a good job as a mother, we parent from a place of worry and apprehension. We fear not being in control. Of course, it is our responsibility as parents to protect our children. But our society is guilty of over-parenting. We are helicopter parents, always there hovering over our children's every step, afraid to let them fall or fail. We won't let them walk down the street in their own neighborhood. We assume that there is a stranger lurking at every playground, ready to snatch our children. Our over-protective parenting is rooted in fear. And not only are we living in fear, but we are also perpetuating fear by becoming a society of tattletale moms. At some point, we have got to trust God with our lives and the lives of our children.

We want to raise a generation of world changers. And, yet, as we continue to parent from a place of fear, we are bringing up a generation that is paralyzed by anxiety. By putting all kinds of undue pressure on our children to succeed, we are teaching them that it's not okay to fail. By refusing to let them out of our sight, we are teaching them that they are incapable of doing anything on their own. We are sending children off to college unable to cope with life. Instead of encouraging them to embrace life, we are causing them to over-think every move. Out of our own insecurities and fear, we are perpetuating more fear. We are breeding fear. Fear is raising fear.

But fear is not from God. As we model this anxiety in parenting, we are teaching our children to see life from a worldview that is not founded in God's peace. We are teaching our children that God is not in control—that we must fight for control. We must stop believing the lies and trust that God is in control. We must teach our children that God is sovereign. Fear is not of God. Fear is from the enemy, Satan. And Satan has us right where he wants us when we live paralyzed by fear instead of living from a place of confidence and freedom as sons and daughters of the King. We want our children to grow up trusting that God is sovereign and that God is good. God is good all the time. The only fear we should know and our children should learn is the reverence, awe, and respect of a holy and just God (Proverbs 9:10). God is holy. We should have a healthy fear of, respect of, awe and reverence in who God Almighty is, but there is no fear in God.

Chapter 13

SOVEREIGNTY OF GOD

SOVEREIGNTY IS DEFINED AS *1) the quality or state of being sovereign, or of having supreme power or authority, and 2) the status, dominion, power, or authority of a sovereign; royal rank or position; royalty.* If we believe that God is sovereign, then we can be at a place of trust, knowing that He has supreme power and authority and is in control. How do we get to that place of trust? Again, it goes back to our worldview. Do we believe that the Bible is the inerrant Word of God? Do we trust that God spoke into existence the entire world and universe? Do we believe that at His word the oceans came into being and the mountains were firmly planted on the earth?

A few years ago I was talking with my cousin, Meg. We had never spent a lot of time together growing up and really only connected in the last few years as adults with families of our own. We quickly learned we had a lot in common in how we parented our children and where we were in our relationship with Jesus. Having not spent much time together, we were comparing stories and trying to trace back and piece together our family of origin. Meg began telling me more about her life story. She was relaying a powerful story about when she gave birth to her son. Within minutes of her son being born, Meg's blood pressure began to drop rapidly. Nurses began frantically trying to assess the situation and called doctors for back-up. Her blood pressure had dropped to 54/25!

By a miracle, Meg was still fully conscious and awake, aware she was being wheeled into the operating room. Meg's life was on the line. She could see the sheer panic and fear on the doctors' and nurses' faces as they raced her down the hall to the operating room. Fully aware she could die, Meg knew that her life and her days were in God's hands and His alone. She calmly began to pray, "Father, bring this medical staff calmness and peace, and allow them to do their job better than they have even been trained, in the name of Jesus!" Although a new mom with a son just minutes old, Meg knew who held her life. Fear had to leave. God is sovereign and in control. A close encounter with death, and yet God spared her life. It was not time for Meg to die.

As I was listening to Meg recount this amazing story, I suddenly stopped her and said, "Wait! This sounds exactly like the story I grew up hearing about my grandfather's wife that did die in childbirth." Meg smiled and nodded.

It was in the midst of conversation, trying to understand the blood lines and the order of maternal and paternal grandparents, that it hit me. Her dad and my mom are only half brother and sister. They have different mothers. My cousin's grandmother had died in childbirth, leaving our grandfather to remarry.

It was like a lightbulb moment when I realized had there not been death, new life would not have occurred. My mom would have never been born had there not been a death in the family, causing

> Nothing is ever wasted
> with God.

my grandfather to meet my grandmother. I would have never been born had there not been death. My cousin and I only exist in having a relationship because there was a death. So often, we live life with a short-sided mentality, not seeing the bigger picture that God is creating.

Although our grandfather experienced the tragic loss of losing his wife in the midst of bringing life into this world, nothing is ever wasted or lost with God. There is no fear when we trust God's sovereignty. With death, we see new life birthed as a part of His masterplan. It doesn't diminish the pain or loss. But the hope we have trusting in the sovereignty of God drives out all fear. We see only what is before us, a small piece of the puzzle; but, God sees the big picture. From our vantage point, we don't always understand or see how God is orchestrating a beautiful masterpiece for His glory. Nothing is ever wasted with God.

It doesn't take long to figure out that there will be many situations in life when our safety or life circumstances are out of our control. Whether it is a natural disaster like a tornado or a display of man's depravity like the 9/11 terrorist attack, scary things will happen. Therefore, we will be put in situations where our children's safety is out of our hands. We can live in fear and be paralyzed by thinking of all the "what if" scenarios of life. We can lock ourselves in our homes, never letting our kids out of our sight and keeping an eye on their every move, or we can live life trusting that God is greater than the circumstances that surround us and He sees the big picture.

Once I began to understand the sovereignty of God, the way I parented changed because I was no longer parenting simply out of fear. And

I was no longer parenting from our culture's worldview because my entire worldview had changed. Although I thought that I trusted God with my girls and my life before, I realized that I had not trusted Him fully and completely. I want that freedom in trusting the sovereignty of God for my girls. I want them to know this kind of confidence that comes from knowing who we are in Christ and trusting that God is fully and completely in control, regardless of what we face in life. We see just a small glimpse, and yet God sees everything as a whole.

In understanding the sovereignty of God, we must come to understand that God is fully in control and that our lives are not about us. We are created to know God and to make Him known. We are created for His glory, not our own. As we begin to take the focus off of "me" and instead make everything we do about Him, peace comes. We can rest in the sovereignty of God, knowing that our purpose and our lives are about knowing our Creator and bringing Him glory. Our lives and stories are for His glory, not our own glory.

> We can rest in the sovereignty of God, knowing that our purpose and our lives are about knowing our Creator and bringing Him glory.

We have to know what we believe and understand that if God Almighty is the author of human life and the Creator of everything we see and enjoy, then He is also able to protect and guide us. Can we trust Him when bad things happen? He is the architect of life. Our days are numbered. Our lives are in His hands. We are not robots, but rather we are created human beings that were created in the image of God and for His glory.

Can we trust that God is sovereign and good and in control in the midst of tragedy and disaster? Can we rest and have peace, putting our trust in a sovereign God? And most of all, can we trust that God is good all the time, regardless of the circumstances we face and the evil that surrounds us? In order to teach our children the love of God in the fallen world we live in, we must first fully know what we believe and why we believe it.

We must get to a place of full surrender. When we understand that life is not all about our own glory and well-being, then we can fully embrace that we were created for one purpose and one purpose only: to live for God's glory. This goes against everything the world says and teaches us to believe. The world tells me that I should be the center of the universe and that my happiness and well-being are all that matter, even if it is at another's expense. But we know that we are not here for our own glory, nor are our children.

We must come to a place where we completely and utterly trust God, no matter what. Our faith must be in Him alone. As the Bible recounts, Job experienced great loss in a short period of time. His servants had been taken and killed. His herds of livestock were destroyed. Then he got word that his sons and daughters had died. This was Job's response: "Naked I came from my mother's womb, and naked I will depart. The Lord gave and the Lord has taken away; may the name of the Lord be praised" (Job 1:21).

These tragedies occurred after God gave Satan permission to test Job. And Satan did his very best, destroying not only Job's livelihood but also taking what mattered most—his family. In spite of it all, Job still remained faithful. In Job 1:22 it says, "In all this, Job did not sin by charging God with wrongdoing." It is this kind of utter dependence and trust in a sovereign and almighty God that occurs when we surrender complete control. While none of us wants to lose our jobs or our loved ones, our trust in God must be unwavering. We must come to a place of total surrender so that, like Job, we can honestly say, "The Lord gives and the Lord takes away, blessed be the name of the Lord."

Are we clinging to our job for security? Are we looking to our husbands to comfort and protect us when only God can truly satisfy? Are we looking to our children to meet our needs and give us an identity instead of God? Have our children become an idol? Do we truly believe that God is sovereign, that He is good, and that He is good all the time? Do we live with that kind of faith, or are we paralyzed and unable to live because of fear?

When God allowed Satan to test Job, He had to grant permission for Satan to even have access to Job. Satan was not allowed to touch Job or anything that belonged to him without God's permission. Job had a hedge of protection around him, and the only access to Job was through God. While we may not understand and may even question why God asked Satan, "Have you considered my servant Job?" (Job 1:8a), we can rest in the knowledge that Satan did not have access unless God allowed it. This gives us a glimpse into the sovereignty of God. As children of God, nothing can touch us without His permission. This means that we can be tested and that we can be in the presence of evil, but God is intensely aware of anything we face or go through and is there for us. It is our job to trust Him in the process. Each trial or testing, struggle or circumstance is God-filtered.

We do not have to walk in fear. Yes, we are in a battle. And, yes, Satan will try to attack. But we do not have to be afraid. We must be securely grounded in who we are in Christ, and we must raise up a godly generation whose foundation is also firmly planted in Christ. We must be intentional in our fight, understanding who the enemy is and how to fight the battle—on our knees and in constant communication with the Maker of the Universe.

> The opposite of fear is resting in the sovereignty of God.

All too often, we are holding onto our children with such a tight grip that it is suffocating. But we must trust God with our children. They are His, after all. He is the giver of the gift. We are just entrusted with them. Are we looking to our husbands to meet a need that only God can satisfy? Are we putting all of our faith in jobs, health, or a lavish lifestyle? If we were to lose it all tomorrow, could we say, "Blessed be the name of the Lord"? Or are we holding on tightly for control? Honestly ask yourself if you have come to a place of complete surrender. For me, it was only when I came to the place where I could fully surrender and genuinely say, "The Lord gives and the Lord takes away, blessed be the name of the Lord" that I found freedom from fear. The opposite of fear is resting in the sovereignty of God.

When we can completely embrace this principle of surrender with our hearts and minds, we can experience the peace that only God can give. It's no longer about me and my fighting for control. I do not exist for my pleasure. I exist for God's glory. We can rest in the fact that, while we do the best we can to protect our children, God cares for them more than we possibly can, no matter how hard we try. We can then confidently embrace our primary purpose as mothers, which is to know our Father God and make Him known to our children.

> Even in the midst of tragedy, we can be confident that God is in control, that He is good, and that our existence is for His glory alone.

Understanding the sovereignty of God puts us in a place of recognizing our frailties and our humanity. It shifts our worldview from the "all about me" mentality to a biblical worldview of God's ultimate control. Whereas the former breeds insecurity and anxiety, the latter grants freedom from fear. Understanding the sovereignty of God allows us to have peace when circumstances occur that are out of our control. Even in the midst of tragedy, we can be confident that God is in control, that He is good, and that our existence is for His glory alone.

We can then safely surrender our children to His care, knowing that He is good all of the time. This is one of the biggest challenges for moms. We want to control and protect our children out of a deep love for them. But as we rest in the fact that God is sovereign and that He is good all the time, our worldview completely shifts to a place of full surrender. The debilitating fear and the need to control are removed, and we can instead focus on who we are in Christ and our purpose for living.

This has been one of the hardest challenges for me, but it has also resulted in one of the most freeing periods in my life. As I mentioned in the last chapter, fear was controlling me to such an extent that it affected the way I parented. Fear can influence the decisions we make as mothers. We become insecure about our kids' safety, about their health, and about every decision we make. We don't want them to go far from home; we want to keep them on a tight leash. We want control. Getting to a place of rest in the fact that God is sovereign and is in control allows a freedom in how we parent our children. And, ultimately, our example presents our children with a compelling reason to trust God and experience a similar freedom for themselves.

I began to understand that as Creator of the universe who spoke the world into existence, He not only has the world under control, but He has my life under control. If He can speak into existence the oceans, control the power of the waves, create mountains, and breathe life into the existence of man, why did I need to live my life worrying or trying to be in control? I began to realize that I was playing God. I wanted to have control, but death is out of my control. And there are many other things that I will face in life that are out of my control. I can do everything in my power to keep my girls safe, but they will still get hurt. I am not God, and yet, I wanted that kind of power and authority. I was assuming that I was so important that my girls needed me—and only me—in their lives. I was assuming that God wasn't big enough to take care of my girls if I wasn't around. I didn't fully trust that God would have the girls' best interests in mind if I wasn't there to oversee the process.

So when our children tell us they want to go to college on the other side of the country or that they want to do a study abroad program or go into missions, we can let them follow the dreams and passions that God has placed in them. If we have done our job well and taught them to pray about every decision, then we can cheer for them instead of holding them back in the tight grip of fear. We can rest in the peace of God and excitedly watch as He fulfills His purposes and plans for their lives.

Allowing our children to grow up trusting in God teaches them to experience the gift of resting in their Father's love. Just as my girls find peace and protection in their daddy's arms at home, I want them to experience that same kind of love and protection as they rest in their Heavenly Father's arms. I want them to be able to go wherever God calls them with a confidence that their protection comes from God and from Him alone. I want them to know and fully understand the sovereignty of God for themselves. I want them to know and experience the father heart of God.

We will face hard times. But can we trust God in the midst of sorrow, pain, and loss? Can we proclaim with bold certainty, "The Lord gives and the Lord takes away, blessed be the name of the Lord"? Does our faith waver, or is our foundation secure? Do we trust that God is good in the midst of pain and tragedy? When we can't see the whole picture, do we still trust His sovereignty? When we can't recognize how God is doing something bigger in our story, do we still have faith that He is working for our good? When the world becomes more and more frightening, do I trust that God still sits on the throne? When terror strikes and evil surrounds me, can I be at peace, trusting God with my children, or do I try to take back that control?

We are not alone in this journey called motherhood. Taking the focus off of myself and fixing my eyes on Jesus shifts my perspective when tragedy strikes. Making it my passion and purpose to know God and make Him known becomes my mission. I do not exist for my glory; I exist for His glory. My children exist for His glory. Resting in the peace that everything is God-filtered and that God is sovereign allows me to parent from a place of peace and not fear. Nothing is wasted on God. He is a good Father. God is sovereign. God is good. God is good all the time. Blessed be the name of the Lord.

Chapter 14

RAISING UP WORLD CHANGERS

MOMS, LET'S BE HONEST. Women are very emotional beings. As a mother of three girls, I firmly believe that PMS starts at age two! When my girls were really young and crying for no reason, this could become frustrating as I attempted to fix whatever was wrong or discover whatever was bothering them. I would try to assess if they were injured or in pain or understand what was making them sad. I would bend down to get on their level, look them in the eye, and ask them what was wrong. I often got a simple, "I don't know." Every woman has been there! I would then ask, "Would you like me to do something for you?" All they seemed to muster was a whispered, "I don't know." I would then try, "Maybe, would you like me to hold you?" Still, "I don't know" was the only answer that I could get. But if I asked, "Would you like some chocolate?" their eyes would open wide, and they would crack a smile as they said, "Okay."

Look, ladies, we all know there are times when we just need a good cry and some chocolate for no apparent reason. Thankfully, I am past the outbursts of emotional toddlers, but since I live in a house full of girls, it is a house that is still full of emotions. I have no medical proof, just experience, and I can definitively say that PMS starts at age two! God made us women to be very emotional beings. Why? I have NO idea! But it does start early.

Possibly, our sensitivity and emotional makeup could be God's way for us to express the nurturing side of His character. We can empathize with our children in a very deep, eternal place that is much different than the makeup and wiring of a father. In His beautifully orchestrated plan, God gave men and women different roles and abilities. He called the man to be the protector and provider, the one tasked with carrying the burden physically for the family. To the woman He gave the honored title of "mother," and He uniquely designed us to physically and emotionally fulfill this amazing calling for our children.

Moms, you are called as a mother. You have been chosen for such a time as this. You have been equipped. You have the opportunity to be a difference-maker in our world today, first to the Jerusalem of our own homes and then to the ends of the earth. As we begin making disciples in our own homes, we are training and raising up world changers. Our family's impact increases, and the potential for global impact grows exponentially when we choose to raise up followers of Jesus Christ in our own homes. Moms, we have influence. We have the opportunity to impact a culture. We have the opportunity to impact a generation and generations to come. Mothers, as we become intentional, we can change the family, which, in turn, can change the world. Moms, we are raising world changers!

The responsibility to discipline, disciple, and influence our children belongs to moms and dads. It is the family, the mother and father, that has been called by God to instruct our children in the ways of Jesus.

> We have the opportunity to impact a generation and generations to come.

It is not the church's responsibility to raise our children spiritually. The church can and should support us, but it is not the church's job or responsibility to raise up a godly generation. The church is a body of believers called to share the good news of Jesus with a lost and dying world, and to encourage one another in the Word of God. The husband and wife have been given the command to be fruitful and multiply. It is the family, a mother and father, who is charged with the authority and responsibility to teach their children about Christ Jesus— when they sit down, when they walk along the road, when they lie down (Deuteronomy 11:19–21).

Our kids will never be perfect. The goal is to create a place in our homes where our children come to know Jesus, have their own experience of who Jesus is, and begin to live out their faith in the world around them. My three princesses are still on the journey. But their precious and tender hearts are soft for Him.

Reagan, our oldest, was recently among a group of peers who were spending a Friday evening together at a friend's house when the conversation among her peers began to decline rapidly. Reagan began to feel uncomfortable in the situation and confronted her peers, using God's Word to defend making wise choices. One of the teenagers began to mock her and challenge her faith. Reagan spoke boldly, confidently defending her relationship with Jesus. The group of peers continued in their misbehavior, at which time Reagan decided to remove herself from the group and return home.

While it is never fun to be made fun of or mocked, learning to not be afraid to be bold about her relationship with Jesus was a real opportunity for Reagan to live out what she believed. Reagan knew that Jesus had already warned us that the world won't understand our love for Him. He told us we would be mocked and hated for our faith and to trust in Him (John 15:18–25). Having had that experience to put into practice what she had been learning from her sweet time of fellowship spent with Jesus has given Reagan more confidence.

Jordan, our middle princess, is in middle school and is learning to navigate friendships. Middle school is hard! While friendships can be like the waves of the ocean coming and going with unknown certainty, being a loyal and faithful friend can be powerful. Jesus is a loyal friend (Proverbs 18:24). At times, Jesus may be the only friend we have. Jordan has recently had opportunities to encourage one of her close friends who was going through a challenging time in her life. Jordan took this opportunity to send her friend frequent text messages in which she typed out Scripture for the friend to dwell on. We can easily become a friend that is ready to listen to the latest gossip or spend hours complaining about how hard a life crisis that we are experiencing is. But being a friend that always points people back to Jesus is a friend that is more interested in encouraging others in their walk with Jesus than in being in the crowds of gossip. Jordan's friend was greatly encouraged with each text message as she relied on the Scripture as a constant reminder that God is sovereign and in control during these trials and challenges being faced.

Becoming a world changer begins with the heart. As our children begin to own the fact that they are not the center of the universe and that the world does not revolve around them, our children see beyond the walls of self. Our culture tells us daily to think only of promoting our own success, bragging about the latest family vacation or event we experienced. But when Jesus begins to rule and reign in our hearts, humility begins to take center stage.

Riley, our youngest princess, is well-liked by all. As we were preparing for her upcoming birthday party, she told me that she really wanted to buy her two best friends a friendship necklace for the three of them to have as a symbol of their friendship. But then she quickly confessed that she would never wear the necklace to school because she would never want anyone else from her class to notice that she had these special friendships and to hurt other peers' feelings. Her heart was tender to the feelings of those around her who may look on in envy. There was much wisdom that came with her willingness to deny herself out of love and concern for others (Proverbs 11:2). Thinking of others and their feelings before self-gratification allowed her to be kind and courteous to her classmates.

> As our marriages and families are intentional to know Jesus, we can make Him known in the way we live.

Our homes are the training grounds for going out into the world around us—to school, the gym, the grocery store, or our job—as the salt and light to a lost and dying world (Matthew 5:13–16). The time and energy required to raise up world changers can be exhausting. But as we become intentional in our own homes and make disciples of our children, when we leave home base every day, every single family member may have the opportunity for impact by sharing the gospel of Jesus to a world that desperately needs Him. As our marriages and families are intentional to know Jesus, we can make Him known in the way we live.

We can neglect one of the greatest places of influence and impact we have been given if we are not careful and purposeful in our calling.

It's like the parable of talents we learn about in Matthew 25:14–30 (ESV). After one man was given five talents, he went out and worked diligently and doubled his talents, earning him ten talents. The man given two talents also worked hard and proudly showed his doubled portion to his master. And then there was the man who was given one talent. He looked around and compared himself to others and felt insignificant and probably unworthy. He assumed that he didn't have what it took to succeed, so he dug a hole and buried his talent, afraid of his master. He just stopped trying. Maybe he felt small and unworthy compared to those who seemingly had more to offer—more experience, more knowledge, more wisdom, more creativity. This man thought that he didn't have a lot to offer. Maybe he was afraid of losing the one talent and disappointing his master, so he thought he would keep it safe and protect it by hiding it in the ground. But he failed to recognize that he had been given something valuable that the master wanted to use in the world. He was not left empty-handed.

Likewise, moms, none of us are left empty-handed either. We have all been apportioned the grace needed in motherhood. But it is out of our own insecurity that we look around at what others have and begin to feel insignificant. We see other moms who are creative and are excellent cooks, those who always look well put together and volunteer at their kids' school, and those who make time for Bible study and friends (all while apparently having an amazing marriage), and we feel inferior. Or we look at all of the scary things happening in the world and in fear hold on tightly to our children and try to shelter them. We take our eyes off what we have been given and begin looking around to what others have and feel unworthy, unqualified, fearful, and lacking. The Bible tells us this is a dangerous place.

The man who buried his talent and felt unworthy to do something with what he had been given was rebuked—harshly. He knew that the master expected a return on his investment. The master expected the talent to be used creatively to bring forth a harvest. It didn't matter how much talent was given; he expected a return because where there is sowing, there is also reaping.

The master in this story is obviously God. Like the master, He gives us all talents and leaves none of us empty-handed. We all have been given something to work with; we all are equipped. Grace has been apportioned. But how often do we take our eyes off Jesus and what He has blessed us with? How often do we take for granted our own individual and unique gifting and instead dwell on either what we don't have or what others do have? There is a shift in our focus. Rather than using the talent that God has given us, we begin thinking that what we have been given isn't enough, that it won't amount to anything, and that those who have been blessed with more are more qualified and have more to offer. We determine that, surely, we aren't worthy, so we bury what we have. We stop trying. We become hopeless.

God rebukes those who bury what He gives because whatever He gives, whether one or ten talents, is still a gift. It is expected to be used. It is expected to be sown. But, remember, while it is our job to sow the seed that God gives us, it is HIS job to take what is sown and reap the harvest. We simply sow the seeds of being faithful to reach our children for Jesus, but it is the Holy Spirit that captures their hearts for Him.

It is not our job to judge or determine if the talent we are given is good enough or qualifies for a successful harvest. He expects us to be faithful to use the talent He gives us. How often as moms do we stand

> We simply sow the seeds of being faithful to reach our children for Jesus, but it is the Holy Spirit that captures their hearts for Him.

in a room and become filled with insecurity? As we look at all the other talents in the room, we suddenly feel unworthy, unqualified, and insignificant. We begin looking for a place to hide and bury the talent we are given. But, moms, we are called. We are all given a talent—some more than others. But we have been called, and we must use the talent God has given and not bury it. The high calling of motherhood is a gift. It is a gift, a talent not to be squandered or wasted or buried.

Our mission as mothers is to reach our children's hearts for Jesus. Our impact has an eternal significance. You have the potential to

> I am a difference-maker. I am a world changer. I am a mom.

directly impact and influence lives. You are holding potential. Don't discard what God has given you, thinking that the role of motherhood is an insignificant or unworthy career. Don't bury your talent. God has called you and equipped you. We were made to thrive, not just survive, in our roles as wife and mother. Let's be mothers who will change the trajectory and go to battle by raising up a godly generation. Moms, you are chosen. You are leaving your mark on history. You are making a difference. You are personally impacting the next generation. Motherhood is the highest of callings. While culture and society has abandoned and orphaned the high calling of motherhood, God has never orphaned or abandoned the high calling of motherhood.

I am a difference-maker. I am a world changer. I am a mom.

WORKS CITED

CHAPTER 1:

@barnagroup. "Tired & Stressed, but Satisfied: Moms Juggle Kids, Career & Identity - Barna Group." *Barna Group.* N.p., 5 May 2014. Web. 27 Sept. 2016.

https://www.barna.org/barna-update/family-kids/669-tired-stressed-but-satisfied-moms-juggle-kids-career-identity#.V4U0LVfO6FI

CHAPTER 2:

Duggan, Maeve, Amanda Lenhart, Cliff Lampe, and Nicole B. Ellison. "Parents and Social Media." *Pew Research Center Internet Science Tech RSS.* N.p., 16 July 2015. Web. 27 Sept. 2016.

http://www.pewinternet.org/2015/07/16/parents-and-social-media/

CHAPTER 3:

"The State of Abortion in the United States." National Right to Life. National Right to Life Committee, Inc., 14 Jan. 2016. Web. 27 Sept. 2016.

http://www.nrlc.org/uploads/communications/stateofabortion2016.pdf

@barnagroup. "Majority of Americans Now Believe in Cohabitation - Barna Group." *Barna Group.* N.p., 24 June 2016. Web. 27 Sept. 2016.

https://www.barna.org/research/family-kids/research-release/majority-of-americans-now-believe-in-cohabitation#.V4W2KFfO6FI

"Cohabitation and Future Marital Stability." *[Marripedia].* N.p., n.d. Web. 27 Sept. 2016.

http://marripedia.org/cohabitation.and.future.marital.stability

CHAPTER 11:

Hunt, Susan, and Yvette Santiago Banek. *My ABC Bible Verses: Hiding God's Word in Little Hearts.* Wheaton, IL: Crossway, 1998. Print.

All Scripture is from the NIV unless otherwise noted.

the *High Calling* of *Motherhood*
STUDY GUIDE

CHIMENE SHIPLEY DUPLER

Available now at retailers online
and at www.ambassador-international.com

For more information about
Chimene Shipley Dupler

and

The High Calling of Motherhood
please visit:

www.facebook.com/chimeneshipleydupler
www.twitter.com/chimenedupler
www.instagram.com/chimeneshipleydupler
To Invite Chimene to Speak: www.passion4moms.org/speaking

For more information about
Passion4Moms
please visit:

www.passion4moms.org
www.facebook.com/passion4moms
www.instagram.com/passion4moms
Contact: info@passion4moms.org
703.957.0405

For more information about
AMBASSADOR INTERNATIONAL
please visit:

www.ambassador-international.com
@AmbassadorIntl
www.facebook.com/AmbassadorIntl